Bow First, Ask Questions Later

Bow First, Ask Questions Later

Ordination, Love,
and Monastic Zen in Japan

GESSHIN CLAIRE GREENWOOD

FOREWORD BY BRAD WARNER

Wisdom

Wisdom Publications
199 Elm Street
Somerville, MA 02144 USA
wisdompubs.org

Library of Congress Cataloging-in-Publication Data
Names: Greenwood, Claire Gesshin, author.
Title: Bow first, ask questions later: ordination, love, and monastic zen in Japan /
    Claire Greenwood; foreword by Brad Warner.
Description: Somerville, MA: Wisdom Publications, 2018. | Includes bibliographical
    references and index. |
Identifiers: LCCN 2017023332 (print) | LCCN 2018007235 (ebook) |
    ISBN 9781614294115 (ebook) | ISBN 1614294119 (ebook) |
    ISBN 9781614293972 (pbk.: alk. paper) | ISBN 161429397X (pbk.: alk. paper)
Subjects: LCSH: Greenwood, Claire Gesshin. | Zen Buddhism—Biography.
Classification: LCC BQ982.R44 (ebook) | LCC BQ982.R44 A3 2018 (print) |
    DDC 294.3/927092 [B] —dc23
LC record available at https://lccn.loc.gov/2017023332

ISBN 978-1-61429-397-2   ebook ISBN 978-1-61429-411-5

22 21 20 19 18   5 4 3 2 1

Cover design by Philip Pascuzzo. Set in Trump Mediaeval LT 9/14.5.
Wisdom Publications' books are printed on acid-free paper and meet
the guidelines for permanence and durability of the Production Guidelines
for Book Longevity of the Council on Library Resources.

♻ This book was produced with environmental mindfulness.
For more information, please visit wisdompubs.org/wisdom-environment.

Printed in the United States of America.

Contents

Foreword

GESSHIN GREENWOOD IS THE REAL DEAL. She's an honest-to-Buddha Zen nun, with the shaven head to prove it. She went through the kind of rigorous training in traditional Zen temple practice that most of the folks you see writing puffed-up fluff pieces for those slick spiritual magazines by the check-out stand at Whole Foods avoided like politicians evading the draft. I certainly never did half the arduous stuff Gesshin managed to do and, amazingly, to somehow survive.

I first met Gesshin at Tassajara Zen Mountain Monastery in Northern California. We were both there doing the summer work-practice thing. That's where they put you to work serving the paying guests who come during the summer to soak in the hot springs and eat gourmet vegetarian food. But work-practice students like us had to follow the monastic schedule and rules. I think we met when we were both shoveling sand into a pit or something.

I was amazed that someone as young as she had such a deep background in Buddhist practice experience. Lots of people you meet at places like Tassajara brag about having done all sorts of cool Buddhist stuff. But when you look into it, it usually turns out they've done all those things they're so proud of for around three hours apiece, like they went and took a class about *vipassana* once, and another time they hung around at the back of a Tibetan Buddhist temple watching the monks cook rice or something. Then they tell the readers of their blogs about how they studied a dozen forms of Buddhist practice.

Gesshin, on the other hand, really did all the stuff. Like, for realsies! She actually immersed herself in Japanese Zen temple life for years doing all the ceremonies, all the services, all the cooking and cleaning and the rest of it. She didn't just attend some "intro to Zen meditation" event so she could tick it off on her résumé of spiritual experiences. She dove all the way into it.

That's what makes this book so valuable. It's rare that someone from the West does any of this stuff, rarer still when they write about it, and yet even more rare that their writing is as good as Gesshin's is. This is a truly unique document of a truly unique lived experience.

BRAD WARNER is the author of *Hardcore Zen: Punk Rock, Monster Movies, and the Truth about Reality* and numerous other books.

1 Welcome to My Tea Shop, Here's a Hot Poker for You

If you do not separate from the monastery for your
whole life, even if you do not speak for five or ten years,
nobody can call you mute.

—DOGEN ZENJI, SHOBOGENZO "GYOJI"

I hate silence when it is time to speak.

—KASSIA, BYZANTINE NUN, NINTH CENTURY

THE LAST WEEK I WAS IN JAPAN, before moving back to America, my teacher gave me Dharma transmission, certifying me to teach Zen, and told me not to tell anyone about it. "Don't announce it," he warned me. "Wait ten years to tell people." Then he gave me his grandfather's *kotsu*, the small wooden staff used by abbots during ceremonies, and told me, "You can teach now." Actually, I don't remember the exact order of things. It's possible that he first gave me his grandfather's kotsu, told me I could teach—and then told me not to announce anything for ten years.

A few days later I was on a plane back to America. The whole event reminded me vaguely of the story of the Sixth Zen Patriarch, Daikan Eno (Huineng, in Chinese), whose teacher transmitted the Dharma to him secretly, at night, and told him to stay hidden for sixteen years until he found the appropriate place to spread the Dharma. There is a long tradition of Zen masters hiding out in secret for years before being discovered by eager students.

Almost a year after Dharma transmission, I have no interest in being the kind of teacher who sits on the high chair in the *zendo*, the meditation hall, and has private meetings with students to test their understanding of reality. On the other hand, I relate a lot to the Zen story about the old lady Zen master who runs a teahouse, making delicious tea for unassuming customers and responding to anyone who asks her about Zen with a hot poker. She's just trying to do her thing, make her delicious tea, run a teashop as old Zen ladies do. Why does everyone have to bug her with questions about *samadhi* and relative and absolute realities? Why don't they just drink their tea?

But despite my grumpy-Zen, old tea-lady attitude, I want to write and share this book. It has been a long journey to get to the point where I could even relate to being a Zen master (or at least a Zen book writer), albeit a grumpy, old, hot-poker-wielding one.

The first time I tried to write this book I was twenty-two years old. The stock market had crashed in 2009, when I was a senior in college, which meant that even if I had wanted a job, there were none. There were no jobs at Starbucks. There were no jobs at McDonald's. Noble low-paying jobs at a nonprofit? Forget it. I was an English major, doing a creative writing thesis that was a collection of love poetry, and so I was even less marketable than I could have been. So I did what any self-respecting, spiritual white girl would have done: I went to India.

India was a short-lived mess—and so I rapidly ended up in Japan, where my college boyfriend, Nate, was studying abroad. He introduced me to Seido Roshi, the monk who would eventually become my teacher; he was also the abbot of a monastery where Nate had spent some time. I stayed for half a year, mostly just trying to wake up at 4 A.M. and keep my head above water. When I couldn't get a visa to stay in Japan, I went back to America and lived with Nate. I was still unemployable, still confused, still lost. Nate didn't want to get married, and I did, but marriage was also the only plan I had, and I knew I was more than that.

It was there, back in America, at age twenty-two, that I tried to write the first draft of this book. I didn't know it was a first draft at the time. It was a novel; it was "fiction" starring an exaggerated version of me: she was brilliant, beautiful, and miserably unhappy, recovering from a nervous breakdown. Nate called her the main "claireacter" because she was so much like me.

It was a good novel. It was sexy and dark. It was intelligent, vulnerable, and kinky, kind of like *Franny and Zooey* meets *Fifty Shades of Grey*. The "claireacter" was drifting through life, too intelligent for her own good, doing all sorts of destructive things to herself and others.

It was a good novel, but I had no idea how to end it. I wrote half a book but got to the point where I had no idea what to do with the character. I didn't want it to be a depressing postmodern novel where nobody changes, where everyone is just as unhappy in the end as in the beginning. I knew I wanted the "claireacter" to grow and become a better person, but I had no idea how to make her do this. I imagined her in different scenarios: moving to France, moving to India, going to therapy, running off with an older man and then recognizing the error of her ways—but I actually had no way of imagining what the emotional growth looked like.

It was then, staring at my computer screen, that I decided to go back to the monastery in Japan. I knew I had to do this because I couldn't even imagine what character development was, not even in a land of total make-believe. I knew that in order to write the kind of book I wanted to write—the kind of book that would help people—I would need to personally change. I would need to grow in such a way that I came to a new understanding of my problems—not that I needed to make my problems go away, but that I needed to come to a way of relating to my problems in a good way.

Ultimately, this is what Buddhism boils down to: learning to relate to yourself and others in a good way, a sane and wise way. It's a way to live life in a good way, in whatever situation you find yourself. That's what I learned, after years of boredom and pain and cold and grief and just the right amount of guidance. I learned how long it takes for things to unfold and develop. I learned how to not give up.

In formal Zen practice this starts small. You deal with the physical objects in your immediate field of vision. You mop the floors and take care of the flowers and practice respectful speech with the people around you. It's very simple and very unexciting. The wonderful part though, the unexpected and amazing part of practice, is that in learning to treat other things well, you learn to treat yourself well. I didn't know this when I decided to move back to Japan, but part of me, maybe my *bodhi mind*, knew that I needed to write this story. So I went back to the monastery in Japan.

I remember sitting zazen in the old zendo, crying from pain and cold. And I remember a voice in my head telling me to stay, to see it through.

THE FIRST TIME Seido Roshi offered me transmission I turned him down. I was about twenty-six years old and was still practicing at Nisodo, the women's monastery where I did most of my training. He thought it would be a good idea to give his three most-senior students transmission at the same time, but I was angry at him for a whole variety of reasons, and so I said no. It took me about three years to get to a place where I knew that yes, this was something I actually wanted, that I could actually face being his student in his lineage forever and for all eternity, which is what Dharma transmission means in Japan: your name is etched into a list of names going back to the historical Buddha, and after that point, you can't erase it or switch lineages. I also knew it would also give me permission to tell my story—and I want to tell my story.

I want to tell my story because I think it will help people, and I have to think that's as good a reason as any. I hope it will encourage and inspire people who are struggling to find their place in the world, who are dealing with difficult emotions—with hopelessness and fear and insecurity. I hope

I can encourage young women in particular because, statistically, we struggle the most with depression and emotional turmoil.

People tell me my writing is funny, so I'm hoping to trick readers into learning something about Buddhism by coating it in humor, kind of like when hippie parents mix kale into their pasta sauce so their kids will eat it without noticing.* In Buddhist terms, mixing kale into the pasta sauce is called *skillful means*. Skillful means are techniques that are not ultimately true but work as expedients. See, you learned a new Buddhist term despite yourself. *Aha!* See what I just did there? Skillful kale for the win!

WHEN I WAS A KID, my favorite books were the ones that involved young girls learning magic or fighting in great battles alongside the boys. Of course I also liked *Little House on the Prairie*, but really I just wanted to read about ten-year-old girls who could talk to animals and shoot fire from their hands. As an adult, there seem to be no equivalent books, no stories about women who are flawed and struggling with demons—both inside and out—but who learn to fight. When you are an adult, where are the women who shoot fire? So I am writing this book because it is what I would want to read myself, what I wish I could have read when I was nineteen years old.

---

*My friend Jon Feyer would like to point out that "kale is cool now!" This is something I missed out on during my years in Japanese monasteries, like the Boston Marathon bombing, the Arab Spring, and the "Gangnam Style" YouTube video. There must be some gross vegetable that is still untouched by the ideals of organic, health-conscious millennials, right? What about chard? Is chard still universally loathed and feared? How about okra?

I started writing this book (again) after I left Nisodo, when I was living on my own for the first time after almost five years of intensive monastic practice. This time it wasn't a novel. I was teaching in a Buddhist studies program, leading meditation classes for American college students, and reflecting for the first time on where my twenties had gone. I came to Japan when I was twenty-three, ordained when I was twenty-four, and left the monastic container when I was twenty-eight, both disillusioned and oddly empowered. This writing reflects that paradox.

There are times when I openly question the tradition, when I am angry or doubtful, and there are times when I revel in it and celebrate it. There are times when I articulate my understanding of the Dharma based on the experiences and perspectives of a nun who has practiced with very traditional Japanese teachers, and there are times when I speak for "myself," when I am informed more by my background as a young American, antiracist feminist, writer, weirdo, etc. Sometimes I sound profound and enlightened, but in those times I am probably just parroting things my teachers have said, which I'm starting to think is what expounding the Dharma is: just one long, cosmic game of telephone. The historical Buddha preached that "all conditioned things are impermanent," and his disciples passed this message down to their students, trying not to change the new message to "conditioner brings tar detergent."

So I hope I haven't written a book about tar detergent. I hope the kale isn't too brittle, and the pasta sauce is not too saucy.

Buddhism is the lens I use to write about and view life,

but my writing isn't only about Buddhism. I hope this comes through. Before I was a Buddhist or a feminist, I was a writer, and before I was a writer, I was a human being. Mostly what I am writing about, to quote William Faulkner, is "the human heart in conflict with itself." Buddhism is my language and my form, the way I have learned to think about and practice being human.

This is all a long-winded way of saying: If you have bought this book to learn about Zen, then you'd better get out of my teahouse because there's a nice red-hot poker waiting for you. But if you'd like to sit and chat and drink tea, then please stay. I'll tell you a story about a young girl on a silly quest for enlightenment, about her many loves, about how she learned to make the best cup of tea in Japan.

So would you like some tea or not?

2   How Water Feels to a Fish

*Sailing beyond the mountains and into the ocean, when
we look around in the four directions, the ocean appears
only round; it does not have any other form at all.
Nevertheless, this great ocean is not round, and it is not
square.... To fishes it is like a palace and to gods it is
like a string of pearls.*

—DOGEN ZENJI, SHOBOGENZO "GENJOKOAN"

IT'S ALL MY PARENTS' FAULT.

If this were therapy, that would be my great break-
through: all my problems, my failed relationships, and the
nun thing—all my parents' fault. Especially the nun thing.
They named me after Saint Claire, and they named my
brother "Gabriel," after the angel Gabriel. And we weren't
even Catholic. They were reformed hippies, and when I was
growing up I didn't watch television and didn't go to church.
I carried my lunch to school in a straw basket. We owned
only four movies: the original *Willie Wonka and the Chocolate Factory*, Disney's *Aladdin*, Mel Brooks's *Spaceballs*, and
this 1970s biopic of Saint Francis of Assisi with a Donovan
soundtrack called *Brother Sun, Sister Moon*. I watched those
four movies—and only those four movies—countless times,
and so the image of beautiful, virginal Saint Claire getting
her head shaved and washing lepers while Donovan music

plays in the background is forever imprinted on my psyche. I mean, who names their daughter "Claire" and then has her watch a movie about Saint Claire over and over again as a kindergartner? Not to mention repeated exposure to Mel Brooks's humor at age seven?! As an adult, my story is a pretty equal composite of those four movies: one part problematic exoticizing of Asian culture, one part sincere yet idealistic spiritual quest, one part cheesy '80s bathroom humor, and one part epic pursuit of candy.

When I was in middle school I became obsessed with Artemis, the Greek goddess of women and the hunt. Artemis is a virgin who swears off men and leads a group of other virginal huntresses. She's usually depicted in a short tunic, carrying a bow and arrow, and she wears a crescent moon on her crown. I thought the idea of living with a bunch of women, running around the forest hunting, wearing a moon crown, and disdaining men was just the best idea ever, and so I was Artemis for Halloween when I was way too old for that to be cute and endearing. My mother made me that costume. So really, it's all my mother's fault.

And now I'm a Zen nun.

PEOPLE OFTEN ASK ME, "How did you decide to become a nun in Japan?" and I never really know what to say. Did I even actually *decide* to become a nun in Japan? I suppose I did, because I knew it was a lifelong commitment. I asked my teacher to ordain me, and he said yes. But it wasn't a long, pained, angsty decision on my part. I didn't make a list of "pros" and "cons" before I decided, because it just felt natural and right. When people ask me how I "decided" to become a nun, or how I "decided" to "join" a monastery in Japan, I've realized that what they're really asking is: How are you? Who are you? Why are you like this? And at least sometimes they're asking: What can I learn from you?

So I would like to invite you to be clear on what your questions are and why you are asking them.

I struggle as a fiction writer because I know that truth is stranger than fiction. There is a novel of experience and emotion in each of our lives—heck, in each of our childhoods—but it doesn't feel extraordinary to us. People tell me it's unusual to move to Japan and ordain when you're twenty-four, but to me this hasn't felt unusual. From my own perspective, everything I've done seems natural; the causes and conditions that led me to becoming a nun in Japan seem unnoteworthy, how water seems like air to a fish. But I will try to explain, as best I can, how I made the decisions I did.

Clearly it's unfair to "blame" my parents, or a few poor movie choices as a child; I look back on the last twenty-nine years for some clues, some crucial, irreparable turning point that forever set my life on course to become a nun in Japan and then live in a convent for years, but I can't find one such isolated incident. What I can sense are one hundred million causes and conditions. There's the trip I took to Italy with my mother when I was twelve, when we stayed in Catholic convents instead of hotels, a trip in which I walked around the convent gardens in some kind of low-grade yet palpable bliss, imagining what my life would be like if I lived there. There's the semester I studied abroad in India in Bodh Gaya, the site of the Buddha's enlightenment, where I actually did ordain temporarily in the Burmese tradition. There's the hours and hours and weeks of time I spent in meditation as a college student, the spring breaks I spent in silent retreat instead of on road trips or in Cancun with friends. There's the creative writing thesis I wrote as an English major that was a comparison between Western notions of romantic love and Buddhist concepts of compassion. And then, when I was a junior in college, one of my best friends, Dave, was killed by a falling tree branch. We were also sleeping together at the time, and he died a few days after I'd flown out to see him. He was out hiking alone when the branch fell on him and broke his neck.

I told this story recently to a high school friend who is one of Thich Nhat Hanh's monks now. (Okay, technically he —my friend, not Thich Nhat Hanh—was my first boyfriend and first kiss in high school, and now he's a monk...look, I don't have weird karma, okay? My life is totally normal!)

He listened to what happened to Dave and said, "Wow, that is really Buddhist."

Which is kind of a fucked up thing to say, right? But he's right, in a way, and I think Dave would agree. Dave was also a Buddhist. We ordained in India at the same time. It's part of why I love India so much.

I resist narrative because I think truth is more compli-cated than one line of points leading to a conclusion. It's easy to say, "Ah yes, Dave was the turning point," but how could there be one turning point? By the time Dave was killed I had already sat hundreds of hours of meditation, already been ordained as a nun in India, already watched a movie of Saint Claire washing lepers' feet a dozen times, already dressed up as a virgin goddess of the hunt with a moon crown for Halloween.

The linguist Roland Barthes wrote a text called *A Lover's Discourse*, which is a love story told entirely out of order, with no plot, in fragments. He explained in the introduction that he wanted to avoid "'a philosophy of love' where we must look for no more than its affirmation." But how do you tell a story that does not leap to an easy affirmation of progress, of growth, of sadness leading to happiness? So far my chosen narrative is: hippie parents, vague Catholic/ spiritual influences, early interest in women's communities and feminism, exposure to Buddhist meditation, international travel, and tragic and random death, which makes me sound like I am a robot making a laundry list of events in my life when I write it like that. I'm a perfectionist, and so I wonder, in telling my story a certain way, am I leaving out another story that could be told? A story where I am sadder, less funny, more normal? A story where I am just selfish and driven by impulse? A story where I haven't grown at all? In choosing to share certain events and claim certain truths, which ones am I leaving out? Which truths am I suppressing?

But I know this is true: at a certain point I did go to Japan.

I HAD A JAPANESE HISTORY PROFESSOR IN COLLEGE. He was a serious Zen Buddhist practitioner and sat a *sesshin* at a temple in Japan in the '90s. This is a fact. It happened.

In class he brought up the temple to his students, and offered to connect anyone interested. My boyfriend at the time, Nate, who was completely disillusioned with academics, took a year off from school to go live in the monastery.

He loved it and went back to Japan a year later on a study-abroad program. After I graduated from college, I worked in India for six months teaching English but became depressed and homesick. I wanted to practice Buddhism deeply, and I wanted a teacher, so it seemed like the best idea was to visit Nate and check out the monastery and teacher he kept raving about.

Just to make sure we're on the same page, this is not the boyfriend turned Thich Nhat Hanh monk, nor is it the man who was a monk with me in India who died. This is a different Buddhist man in a monastery.

Like I said, I don't have weird karma with men and Buddhist monks...

Stop looking at me funny.

3   # What's Authentic about
      # Japanese Buddhism?

[There's] a stage in Buddhism that is called "bright faith," which is like falling in love. It's as though we've been looking at a door that seems to have been shut forever, and then it opens.... Now, strangely enough, the path from bright faith to verified faith is by way of doubt—doubting and wondering and questioning and exploring.

—SHARON SALZBERG, *FAITH*

I REMEMBER ARRIVING IN JAPAN from India and thinking I was in heaven. The streets were clean and no one talked to me. After the constant hassle and noise of India, this was a huge relief. Nate and I stayed in bed for days, emerging only to make quick trips to the massively large grocery store on the corner to buy beer and cheap sushi. But despite the joy at being together after six months apart, there was, as usual, the pull to move on to the next thing, the next trip, the next experience. I was twenty-two years old.

Eventually we took a long, slow, local train ride to Toshoji, an old monastery in Okayama prefecture. I was given a black meditation robe and a room to share with an Australian nun, and told to follow the schedule. Nate introduced me to the

abbot of Toshoji, a short, clean-shaven monk named Seido
Suzuki Roshi. Initially I thought he was completely unremarkable. The more I got to know him, however, the more
I began to think that there could be no human on the planet
as unremarkable as he—and this made him (paradoxically)
remarkable indeed.

Nate went back to school and I continued on with the
small group of monks and nuns. We would wake up at 4
A.M. and go to the cold zendo to sit in meditation, zazen.
After two fifty-minute periods of zazen, the monks put on
their *okesas*, the patchwork mantles worn by monks to
symbolize their renunciation, and filled the Buddha hall
for chanting services. As we chanted, it was so cold that we
could see our breath, and our hands became stiff holding
the books.

During service every morning I watched Seido Roshi bow
in front of the altar, lifting up his okesa gently so it didn't
touch the floor and then dropping to the ground, kneeling
until his forehead touched the bowing mat. He bowed over
and over, for every ancestor and former abbot's name we
recited, and when he bowed I could see the balls of his feet
sticking out from under his robe. They were almost blue
with cold, the skin cracking. And yet his movements were
filled with a quiet dignity and sincerity. I couldn't look away.

In Japanese, we call the mind that seeks awakening
bodaishin (in Sanskrit, *bodhicitta*). The word combines
the character for awakening or enlightenment, *bodai*, 菩提,
with *shin*, 心, the character for heart and mind. This is the
mind that calls us over and over to the meditation cushion
or to meditation retreats, despite loneliness or the pain in

our legs. This is the mind that asks questions about reality and about our own suffering. And it is also the mind that wants to awaken all sentient beings. Dogen Zenji wrote, "To establish *bodhi mind* means to vow and to endeavor that, 'Before I myself cross over, I will take all living beings.'"

Sometimes meeting a teacher or spiritual friend awakens or reenergizes bodhi mind. We see in them a direction or trajectory, and this gives form and shape to our questions and spiritual longing. It's helpful to have someone to look up to, to show us how far we can go, to encourage us when we feel like giving up.

Seido Roshi didn't speak much, but just watching him move made me want to learn from him. I remember one day he came into the kitchen, where I was cooking lunch, and asked how it was going. I told him I didn't know how to cook beans and he laughed and said, "It's not difficult, I'll show you." He stood beside the stove where I was boiling beans, opened a bag of sugar, and stuck a spoon inside. Slowly, carefully, he dumped one spoonful of sugar into the pot, then stood with the spoon suspended over the pot for a moment, waiting. I couldn't take my eyes away from this simple action. He repeated the motion, adding another spoonful of sugar, then another. His whole body and mind were absorbed in the task of pouring sugar; no energy was wasted. Whatever made someone move like that, I wanted it.

And I wanted to be around him all the time. Some of my happiest memories of Japan are of working in his house, cleaning the kitchen or making him tea while he worked or drew calligraphy in long, black strokes. Eventually we would pause, eat cookies and drink coffee, and talk until a monk or visitor came on official business and we had to pretend to be working instead of chatting.

I PRACTICED AS A LAYPERSON at Toshoji for half a year, and then (when I couldn't get a visa) I went back to the United States for a few months. It was at that time, trying (and failing) to write a novel, that I decided to come back to Japan for good, or at least for a very long time. I had moved from a cold, dark monastery to Hawaii, of all places, where Nate was doing research, but despite the warmth and beauty of the island, all I could think of was going back to Toshoji. I just wanted to practice, to sit in silence. I wanted the cold and the dark and the smell of incense and the plain rice porridge we ate for breakfast. When I finally did get a visa and made it back to Japan, I immediately asked Seido Roshi to ordain me.

Sixth months later, after sewing a blue okesa, I ordained on December 28, 2010.

AFTER TEN MONTHS OR SO, practicing as a nun at Toshoji, I decided to move to an all-women's monastery, called Aichi Nisodo, run by a nun named Shundo Aoyama Roshi.

I ended up practicing there for about three years. I didn't really start asking questions about what I was doing until about a year or so into my stay at Nisodo, a year and a half after ordaining. Yet it slowly dawned on me that I had lost all my hair, lost my boyfriend, lost my friends, and essentially lost my family.

I guess *lost* is a misleading word, because, after all, I chose to give them up. I had given up all these things, and for what? Nisodo is very strict, and nuns can be very mean to each other. It's very little sleep and a lot of work in an intense, hierarchical environment, and there's actually very little zazen, so at some point I began feeling like I had lost sight of my initial motivation to practice. The flame of bodhi mind, which had been so strong as to inspire me to ordain, had now diminished to embers.

When I decided to leave the monastery and work on a study-abroad program, my doubts only increased. I started to ask myself, almost on a daily basis, "What am I doing in Japan?" The emphasis of this question shifted around, depending on my mood. Sometimes the emphasis was on the "what" of "What am I doing?" Other times it was on the "I" or on the "doing." But the most common emphasis was on "Japan." What was I doing in *Japan*?!

If you hadn't figured it out from my robotic laundry-list narration of my life, I never had a special interest in Japan. Some Americans grow up loving anime and Pokémon, and for them Japan is a paradise of J-pop and Godzilla. Other people are attracted to the aesthetics of traditional Japanese culture and arts—to haiku, empty spaces, bamboo, paradoxical phrases, tea ceremony, martial arts. And while I do enjoy a clean, empty tatami room or a bamboo forest as much as the next gal, that's not why I went there. I went because, like most young people, I was in search of answers. I heard there was a good teacher in a monastery there, and so I went.

Of course, I didn't find answers. I just found more and more questions and doubts.

But actually that's okay.

I WANT TO WRITE ABOUT THE WORD "AUTHENTICITY," about how much I hear this word and how confused I am by it, and also why I can't help myself from wanting to use it.

I've heard a couple Westerners tell me that they came to Japan to practice Zen "at the source," the implication being that Japan is the source of Zen, and so practicing in Japan, by proximity or osmosis, puts them closer to "true Zen" or "true Buddhism." I imagine this kind of attitude may have been more prevalent in the '60s and '70s, when Westerners were first getting into Zen and had absolutely no idea about the realities of Zen practice in Japan. Maybe people are a bit more informed these days.

There is some understanding about the economic realities Japanese priests face and the decisions they have to make about their livelihoods and families. When I was at Tassajara (a Zen retreat center associated with the San Francisco Zen Center), quite a few students I talked to mentioned how "the only thing monks do in Japan these days is own funeral parlors," which is a kind of funny distortion of the facts; I don't know a single monk who owns a funeral parlor. Funeral parlors are privately owned businesses. Families pay a fee to the funeral parlor and also to the priest they hire, who is not necessarily connected with the funeral parlor. But I digress. The point is that, as more and more firsthand accounts and literature about Buddhist history becomes available, people are starting to doubt whether Japan is the "source" of Zen they always dreamed it was.

Yet, despite some explicit cynicism and criticism by Westerners about Japanese practice, it seems that at the core of this cynicism is a deep longing for "authenticity," both for an "authentic" Buddhist practice and authenticity with themselves. I can't blame anyone for this. I want "true" Buddhism or "true" Dharma practice as much as the next person. Yet over the years, I've stopped being able to ignore exoticism and unfounded idealism when it manifests in me and when I see it manifesting in others. I saw this coming up for me especially when I was the teaching assistant on a Buddhist study-abroad program, working with a group of twenty-year-olds who were in Japan for the first time, bringing with them their dreams and hopes about Buddhism. I am a huge cheerleader for Japanese Zen, but I wanted them to see Japanese Buddhism for what it was, not for what they wanted it to be.

I started to see the exoticism and idealism in myself when I began practicing at Nisodo. At the time there were two other Westerners and more than twenty Japanese nuns. Nisodo is extremely hierarchical, and you are expected to be obedient to your seniors at all times. So for the first few months, that's everyone. You have to obey everyone. When Japanese nuns would give me an instruction or even a harsh criticism, I would jump to obey or correct myself. But when one of the two Westerners corrected me, a thought would flash through my mind like "What do you know?" or "Who are you to be correcting me?"

I didn't trust that they knew about monastery life or about Buddhism, because they weren't Japanese.

Several years later, when I started to be in a position of seniority, I quickly learned that it was useless to try to instruct Westerners when they first arrived. For the most part, the Westerners who came to Nisodo didn't want to listen to corrections from other Westerners. They wanted to learn from Japanese people. And again, I can't really criticize this because I did it too. Why come all the way to Japan just to have some French nun tell me how to bow? The underlying assumption or bias or dream is that Japanese people naturally are more in tune with Buddhism. They are more "authentic."

SCHOLARS AND ACADEMICS have basically done away with the notion of cultural "authenticity." Cultural authenticity implies the existence of an essential, monolithic culture that doesn't change—and of course cultures and people are always changing. The same is true, I think, of Dharma practice. In recent years, scholars have rejected the notion that a "Golden Age" of "Pure Chan" existed in China, where monks single-mindedly pursued koans under the guidance of an inscrutable master, untouched by involvements in economics, politics, ritual, and magic.

People have also recently begun to question the alleged "purity" of Dogen's Zen, the teaching at the heart of the Soto school of Zen. We don't know so much about Dogen, actually—but we know he had donors and supporters, and somehow, money had to have been involved somewhere. I'm not sure we can say that Dogen's Zen was "pure" in the sense that it was entirely unmixed with worldly desires. He was, after all, a human. In the case of humans, desires are inexhaustible.

I don't think the word "pure" is very useful.

Still, if there is no such thing as "authenticity" or "purity," why did I stay so long in Japan? What was I doing there? I'm pretty sure now that it was more than romantic, idealistic notions about the authenticity of Japanese Buddhism. But what? Why didn't I practice in America, where I could have eaten bread, slept in a real bed, and had a boyfriend in the process? Did I practice in Japan because I felt it wouldn't be "real practice" if I had these things? Am I defining "real practice" to myself as the absence of comfort and independence? Did I really need to be in Japan for that? My question actually isn't a new one.

For any of us, why go anywhere at all?

It's clear to me that there is something unique about the experience of practicing Zen in Japan. Part of it might be that because Buddhism is so old and deeply engrained in Japanese culture, it's easier for monastics to be supported there. It could be that as Buddhism becomes more rooted in Western culture, as we develop more Buddhist universities, wealthy Buddhist patrons, and large, established monasteries, it will render going to Asia to practice Buddhism unnecessary.

4   The Thing Itself

the thing I came for:
the wreck and not the story of the wreck
the thing itself and not the myth

    —ADRIENNE RICH

W<small>HEN</small> I <small>WAS AROUND FIVE OR SIX YEARS OLD</small>, I started asking my parents whether things were "true" or whether they were "real." In my five-year-old brain, these were separate categories, and I needed them to make sense of things that affected my emotional reality but had a dubious existence in the physical, material world—things like fairy tales (true but not real), Santa Claus (true but not real), arguments (real but not necessarily true), and giant winged, metal machines that allow you to fly through the sky (real but unbelievable).

It's clear to me that I am still asking these same questions. What is the most real? When I first came to Japan I wanted to know about reality, but I was more enthralled with a dream of Zen, a dream of enlightenment. What I saw reaffirmed and encouraged my dream: bamboo trees, bells tolling in the evening, snowy mountains, and monks with shaved heads. I sat for hours and hours unmoving in a cold zendo trying to understand, what is Buddha?

I begged for food in the snow as part of the ceremonial begging practice organized by the monastery, and I wrote poems about plum blossoms.

The other day I found not one but three videos I had taken on my old camera of rain falling in the monastery courtyard. I was dreaming a beautiful dream about Zen, but eventually I woke up.

Now there's no special "Zen rain" to me.

There's just rain.

I remember a turning point I had about Zen and enlightenment. I was in my teacher's room, and he was preparing to go to an important funeral at another temple. He asked me to iron one of his okesas, which was a bright gold color. It must have been early in my stay, because I still didn't understand what transmission was or what the different colors of okesas meant. When I picked up his okesa I asked him the meaning of the gold color, and he told me that it meant he'd received Dharma transmission from his teacher.

At the time I thought this meant he was fully enlightened and a big deal. I didn't know that Dharma transmission in Japan is mostly patrilineal, from father to son, in order to secure temple inheritance. And I didn't believe what I do now—that transmission marks the progression and completion of certain benchmarks in training, both spiritual and psychological, but also political and bureaucratic.

I then inquired about the other monks I'd seen who wore gold okesas.

He told me that they too had all received transmission.

At that time I'd been getting bullied by one of the Japanese monks in the monastery. I didn't understand about Japanese culture or monastery life yet and was getting things wrong constantly, and so he was always yelling at me. At one point he'd actually picked me up by the collar of my shirt and screamed at me because I hadn't closed a door when someone asked me to. I managed to run away to my room and shut the door, where I sat in a chair kind of hyperventilating. The women lived in a separate building and men weren't allowed to enter, but he actually followed me, opened the door to my room, and continued yelling at me until some other monks came around and restrained him.

I was still reeling from this event when I had the conversation with my teacher about transmission. The monk who'd picked me up and screamed into my face wore a gold okesa, meaning he also had transmission. When I listened to my teacher's explanation and everything finally clicked in my head, I started to cry. I shed tears over my teacher's gold okesa because it didn't mean anything anymore. Or, maybe it still meant something but not what I wanted it to mean. Not what I'd hoped and dreamed about.

ACCORDING TO ONE SURVEY, more than 80 percent of Buddhist clergy in Japan are married and "80 percent of clerics inherited their temples from a family member." This means that the vast majority of Buddhist clergy receive transmission from their fathers. It's easy to see why people would look at this sort of situation and write off transmission in Japanese Zen as "not real." There are definitely Zen teachers who want to "make transmission real again." Apparently Shunryu Suzuki Roshi was like this. Part of why he wanted to work with Westerners was he felt that Japanese

Buddhism was corrupt and he wanted to revitalize it and make transmission "mean something real."

Even Otani Tesuo, the president of the Soto Zen university called Komazawa, wrote in an essay called "To Transmit Dogen Zenji's Dharma" (from a book called *Dogen Zen and Its Relevance for Our Time*):

> We in the Soto school need to seriously reflect on the appropriateness of the contemporary state of Dharma transmission in Japan. Reflecting on both Dogen's own understanding of Dharma transmission as well as the Edo-period commentators, we must take a hard look at the reality of the situation today and ask ourselves whether the custom of familial inheritance of temples is really appropriate. It is a perfect opportunity for us to reflect on the real meaning of what it means to transmit the Dharma.

Otani Tesuo wanted to make transmission more real—but I have to ask the same thing I've been asking since I was five: What do you mean when you say "real"?

How is getting transmission from your father any less real than receiving it from a nonrelative you've practiced with for several years and you call your teacher? Where is our idea of "real" coming from? Is it based on some idea about attaining realization? Or understanding? If so, understanding what? If the Buddha Way is unsurpassable, how can we say at any point that we have sufficient "understanding"? How is basing transmission on "understanding" any more real than basing it on family inheritance? Moreover, how is basing transmission on "understanding" any more "real" than basing it on nothing?

It's interesting to me that people these days are talking about revitalizing Buddhism and returning it to its roots, because it seems people have been wanting to do this for as long as there's been Buddhism. When Eisai, who is credited with founding Rinzai Zen, went to China, he was looking to rejuvenate Buddhism and bring it back to a pure state. That was in the twelfth century. I read a critique of the practice of *shuso hossenshiki*, or Dharma combat, written all the way back in the Tokugawa period (1603–1868). Dharma combat is a ceremony in which the head monastic practitioner receives Dharma questions and is meant to give responses on the spot. The anonymous author lambastes Soto Zen monks for staging Dharma combats instead of answering questions spontaneously. This criticism of overemphasis on form is still going on today. "Real" Dharma combats are supposed to be spontaneous, but in Japan, everyone learns the questions and memorizes responses beforehand.

At Nisodo nuns would sometimes talk about "in theory" versus "in reality." For example, in theory, the head monk is a senior trainee who is a good example for others. In actuality, there are only about thirty-one training monasteries in Japan, and thousands and thousands of monks who need to be head monk to qualify to own a temple, so there just isn't enough space for everyone to fulfill this role in that way. Monasteries have to create special opportunities for monks and nuns to be head monk during shorter, special practice periods. In theory, the head monk would be as mature as a teacher and answer spontaneous questions about the Dharma, but in reality the Dharma combats are performed by young priests and are rehearsed.

My own experience of being head monastic was that, even though I was not the most senior, and even though my Dharma combat was mostly scripted ("not real"), it still was very meaningful. It just wasn't meaningful in the way I wanted or expected it to be. The meaning for me was not about me showing how mature and advanced I am as a practitioner. It was actually the opposite. For me, the meaning was about realizing that I am a very, very small part in a much larger tradition, and that at all times I depend on dozens of other people to help, teach, support, and encourage me.

So which is more real, the theory or the fact? Is a beautiful dream about Dogen's Zen and authentic Dharma practice more real than what is actually happening? Or is the dream more real because it's Dogen's dream that he's inviting us to dream with him?

Maybe they're not mutually exclusive. Maybe I can be in touch with the dream but still be awake to reality, but I don't really know how to do that anymore. I do think spiritual authority should be based on understanding. But for myself, I don't feel comfortable encouraging myself to pursue a special kind of understanding. In my experience, seeking special understanding is privileging a dream. So even though I want to practice "real Dharma practice," do a "real" head monk ceremony, and receive "real transmission," I can't help but think there's nothing more "real" than what's really going on.

5

Bow First,
Ask Questions Later

The bhiksuni Utpalavarna...goes into the houses of nobles and constantly praises the method of leaving family life, saying to all the aristocratic ladies, "Sisters! You should leave family life."

The noblewomen say, "We are young and our figures are full of life and beauty. It would be difficult for us to keep the precepts. Sometimes we might break the precepts."

The bhiksuni says, "If you break the precepts, you break them. Just leave family life!"

They ask, "If we break the precepts we will fall into hell. Why should we want to break them?"

She answers, "If you fall into hell, you fall."

—DOGEN ZENJI, SHOBOGENZO "KESA-KUDOKU"

I LOVE THE PRECEPTS, the moral and ethical teachings of Buddhism, and I have taken them several times.

My nun friend at Nisodo pointed out to me that "receiving" the precepts is a better word to use than "taking," so I am trying to make an effort to change my language. I've received the precepts many times in different traditions, and the first time I did, in the Tibetan tradition, I didn't give them so much thought.

Lots of Westerners especially are very intentional and conscious about receiving the precepts, and the ceremony is something they choose to do after a long time of practice and consideration. But for me, as soon as I started practicing Buddhism, precept ceremonies were always something I naturally wanted to do. This is probably why I ordained very young, without deliberating about it so much. When we receive precepts, we are affirming our basic goodness, and since this basic goodness is available to us at all times, it makes sense that the desire to receive precepts occurs naturally, without so much thought or psychological processing.

Once I was chatting with a Buddhist friend, and I kept making jokes about how I was breaking precepts—by gossiping, for instance, which isn't technically a precept violation in the Soto Zen tradition (but is in others). Over the course of the conversation, I kept adding to the list of my imagined precept violations.

"Sorry," I said finally. "I actually don't know what the precepts are."

"That's because you took the precepts in gibberish," he said.

I was miffed.

I've received the precepts four times in gibberish: twice in Japanese and twice in Tibetan (from Tibetan rinpoches in America and India, when I was in college).

The precepts are something we work with and evolve, break and renew, ingest and digest, and on a very personal, individual level, language matters. Accordingly, I think saying the precepts in our own language (or at the very, very least, understanding what we are saying) matters a great deal.

But in another sense, I don't think language matters so much. The hard-line, conservative view of the precepts is that it doesn't matter if you're aware of the meaning or not; it doesn't matter if you believe in them or not. As in zazen you sit, and this is in itself enlightenment. Sutras abound with descriptions about how simply the act of receiving the precepts is the basis of our enlightenment. In this view, receiving the precepts does the work for you. There's some doctrinal debate about this, of course. According to Buddhist studies professor William Bodiford in *Zen and the Art of Funerals*:

> Kyogo [Dogen's disciple]…argued in the traditional Tendai fashion that the bodhisattva precepts are not merely precepts but actually embody the essence of the Buddha. Kyogo asserts that in contrast to the [Theravadan] precepts, which just control our karmic actions, the Mahayana bodhisattva precepts describe Buddha nature (i.e., reality) itself. The Mahayana precept "not to kill" should be interpreted not as a vow against killing, but as a realization of living enlightenment that clears away the "dead," static entities of our illusions.

This is pure esoteric-mumbo-jumbo gold. All this time I thought I was just vowing not to kill mosquitos… Turns out it's not about not killing but about not needing to not kill because I'm already enlightened… Screw you, mosquitos! Wait, what? Ugh. That's not right.

The more I read about the religious culture Dogen was born into, which was heavily steeped in an esoteric view of original enlightenment (as articulated by William Bodiford's explanation above), the more I understood how I could have been allowed to receive the precepts in Japan (and even ordain) without actually knowing what I was saying.

I should mention that the precepts are the same whether you are ordaining as a layperson or as a monk/nun/priest, receiving Dharma transmission, getting married, or are dead and somebody is doing your funeral. It's all the same precepts. But what I am talking about below is my first encounter with the sixteen bodhisattva precepts as a layperson. This is my story.

ABOUT FOUR MONTHS INTO MY STAY AT TOSHOJI, I was told there would be a "sewing sesshin" during which we would sew our *rakusus* all day for a week. (A rakusu is the bib-like garment representing the Buddha's own robe; it's a miniature version of the okesa, the mantle that monks wear.) I dutifully showed up and sat down. A couple of old ladies from the village had been invited to come help us. There was some chanting and bowing, and then somebody handed me a few small pieces of black fabric and taught me how to sew backstitch. For a few days I just sewed the pieces like I was shown, alongside a bunch of really cheerful old Japanese women who laughed merrily at my terrible stitch work.

A few days later, one of the resident nuns mentioned that I would probably take *jukai*, since I was sewing a rakusu. I did not know what that was.

One evening I was washing the dishes in the kitchen when Seido Roshi manifested next to me, drying dishes. I'd never seen him do that before, and I think I never saw him do that again, but there he was, busily wiping down plates and bowls.

Eventually he asked me, "Do you want to do jukai?"

"What's that?" I asked.

He said, "Receiving the precepts."

"I've already taken the precepts from another teacher, is that okay?"

"Yes."

"Okay," I said.

And that was that.

I assumed there would be some kind of formal teaching or class about the meaning of the precepts, but there never was.

A few days before the ceremony was supposed to take place, I marched to the abbot's room and knocked on the door. He let me in and made me tea. I asked him to explain the meaning of the precepts. He scrunched up his face and winced.

"Hmm, very difficult to translate," he said.

He pulled out a book in Japanese and started leafing through it. "Hmm, too difficult to translate. Why don't you ask Hobai?" Hobai was an American man who had practiced at Zen Mountain Monastery and could read classical Japanese.

I asked Hobai for the meaning of the precepts, and he printed them out from the website of Zen Mountain Monastery.

The Sixteen Bodhisattva Precepts

The Three Treasures

I take refuge in the Buddha
I take refuge in the Dharma
I take refuge in the Sangha

The Three Pure Precepts

Not creating evil
Practicing good
Actualizing good for others

The Ten Grave Precepts

Affirm life; do not kill
Be giving; do not steal
Honor the body; do not misuse sexuality
Manifest truth; do not lie
Proceed clearly; do not cloud the mind
See the perfection; do not speak of others' errors and faults
Realize self and other as one; do not elevate the self and
    blame others
Give generously; do not be withholding
Actualize harmony; do not be angry
Experience the intimacy of things; do not defile the
    Three Treasures

I took one look at this and said, "These aren't the *real*
precepts."

By the way, sometimes I can be kind of a brat...

By "real" I of course meant "Japanese." Japanese = real.
Obviously.

Hobai sighed and very kindly spent the next several days
translating the precepts for me from the classical Japanese.
When he finished he handed me a piece of paper and laughed,
"There you go! No sex, no sake."

That's basically the language that's used. Don't kill. Don't lie. No sex. No sake.

Concerned, I stopped the abbot in the hallway. I think I was really thinking about sex, but I asked about alcohol.

"I don't think I can stop drinking alcohol," I said.

"Well, don't drink too much," he offered.

That was the best explanation I ever got. That was the teaching about precepts. The night before the ceremony, I turned in my rakusu to the abbot to sign and authorize.

I had sewn my rakusu at the same time as an older, Japanese monk, who vehemently hated sewing, and so he had left most of the sewing to the old Japanese ladies. Because of this, his rakusu was really well made. Not knowing the backstory, the abbot assumed that the better-quality rakusu was mine,* so he wrote my name on the Japanese monk's rakusu and gave my rakusu to the monk. The rakusu I wear today is actually the rakusu of a middle-aged Japanese monk named Jitsugai.

Seido Roshi gave me a new name, Gesshin, which means "moon mind."

LOOKING BACK ON THIS EXPERIENCE, I realize now that the precepts ceremony I had (and later, the style in which I ordained) reflects the Japanese style of Zen training that I call "Bow first, ask questions later." There is a different understanding of ceremony and ritual in Japan because, in Japanese, there is no equivalent word for *ritual* or *ceremony*. The closest word to *ceremony* is *gyoji*, 行持, which combines the characters for "go" or "do" with the character for

---

*Because I'm a girl, and girls are good at sewing and are made of sugar and spice and everything nice?

"maintain." It really means something closer to "event." So in a monastery context, gyoji is anything that you do. Things that fall under the category of gyoji in a Japanese monastery are chanting, sitting zazen, taking a bath, eating, or receiving the precepts.

In the Japanese context there is an understanding that participating in the ceremony—such as a precept ceremony or ordaining—itself has meaning, that the ceremony engenders the vow and practice through embodying form, not the other way around. In the West, we usually approach the precepts as promises we make first, bolstered and strengthened by the precept ceremony; in the West, receiving the precepts is descriptive, rather than prescriptive.

But this was never my experience in Japan. People receive transmission at an earlier age as well, because there's an understanding that by embodying the form of someone who has been transmitted—wearing a brown okesa, doing *zuise* (being abbot-for-a-day at Soto Zen's head temple)—you grow into the role. This style of practice reflects Dogen's understanding of the unity of practice and realization (also translated as "experience," which is a problematic translation, since the word *experience* is a word that entered the Japanese vernacular only in the nineteenth century). In the "Bendowa" (Talk on the Wholehearted Practice of the Way) chapter of Shobogenzo, Dogen wrote, "In the Buddha Dharma, practice and experience are completely the same.... This is why the Buddhist patriarchs teach, in the practical cautions they have handed down to us, not to expect any experience outside of practice."

Japanese monastic practice purposefully collapses the

distinction between ceremony and meaning, between bodily form and understanding, in order to arrive at something close to the unity of practice and realization. This is why receiving the precepts in a ceremony, no matter what your mind is doing, is seen as more important than believing or thinking about the precepts. In this way, I think the Japanese style of Zen practice is closer to Dogen's articulation of the unity of practice-enlightenment.

The Japanese style is closer to Dogen's intention, but it's also more challenging, and there is greater room for failure—for producing mean and ill-spirited practitioners. There is little space for confusion or doubt. Form is privileged over emotional or psychological processing. There is an understanding that embodying correct form is the same as having correct view.

The day before I ordained as a nun, I asked Seido Roshi, "What does it mean to be a nun?"

He said, "You'll know after you become one."

Bow first, ask questions later.

6   Buddha Never Told Me to Be Stupid

When Priest Yaoshan was sitting in meditation a monk asked,

   "What do you think about, sitting in steadfast composure?"

   Yaoshan said, "I think not thinking."

   The monk said, "How do you think not thinking?"

   Yaoshan said, "Non-thinking."

   —*THE TRUE DHARMA EYE: ZEN MASTER DOGEN'S 300 KOANS*

I'd like to see a show of hands, please. Who here has ever made a mistake you regretted?

   —MONICA LEWINSKI

AFTER ORDAINING I WENT with Seido Roshi everywhere. He would take me to funerals and memorials, to large branch temples, to Tokyo on business. I was his shadow, but I also loved him very deeply. What started out as me admiring him as a teacher eventually progressed to falling in love with him—and this would have been a relatively minor problem if he hadn't loved me back.

   I don't want to write in detail about this at this point in my life because it is personal and very painful and because—despite being strong and resilient and valuing honesty—there are some things that are just too hard to share.

What I will say is that the feeling I am left with—when I think of him, and myself, at age twenty-something—is profound sadness. I'm sad that I lost my teacher, and I'm sad that I lost my community. Because even though I still call him my teacher, and even though I received transmission from him, something was lost forever when I saw up close the ways in which he was incapable of escaping from his conditioning, the way he could hurt me without realizing. He stopped being able to view me objectively—that is the saddest part.

I'm sure there's anger too, but what's most immediate is sadness at that loss.

I eventually decided to leave because staying was impossible. I wanted to grow up, to practice more seriously, and I knew Seido Roshi's monastery was not the place for me to do this.

I remember sitting beside my Dharma sister in the sewing room, after I had decided to leave. "It's almost poetically tragic," she said. "How you two are with each other."

"Almost," I thought. Things don't feel poetically *anything* when the life you know is crumbling around you.

FOR THOSE OF US who engage in rigorous spiritual practice, the journey will often be a negotiation of boundaries. The relief that Buddhist practice brings, after all, is loosening our grasp on the small self; we find that we can separate from our personal views, and this brings tremendous peace of mind. So in the beginning of practice, thrilled by the potential of separating from our ego, many of us are willing to give up large chunks of our personality or identity. And yet, the more we progress down this path, the better we get at understanding when the sacrifices being asked of us are too much, when endurance is hurting rather than helping. We become more skilled at understanding what our best self needs. Paradoxically, we learn that by establishing firm boundaries, we can be more giving and genuinely altruistic.

In the Zen tradition especially, there is a lot of emphasis placed on "not thinking." In "Fukanzazengi" (Universal Instructions for Zazen), Dogen Zenji wrote, "Think of not-thinking. How do you think of not-thinking? Non-thinking. This in itself is the essential art of zazen." Most teachers of Zen, in Japan at least, will tell you that Zen is "not about thinking," and that practice is something that you do primarily with your body. This is pertinent advice for Westerners especially, who seem to come in with lots of intellectual questions they want to answer, and seem less willing to clean the floor and sit silently for ten years. So generally the advice given is to just practice without trying to understand what's happening, because the only way to actually learn something is to engage with the thing itself without adding your own idea. If you add your own idea, then you're just engaging with your idea, and not the thing you're trying to learn.

I should add that this is all advice I've personally received.

I'm always trying to add my own idea. To this day, sometimes in the monastery when I get presented with work, formal ceremonies, or a list of Buddha names to memorize, I think, "This isn't right. This isn't Buddhism." Thankfully I've gotten better and better over the years at letting go of that idea and accepting what is happening, accepting that there is teaching and meaning in all situations, and that I probably won't know what the meaning is until I do it. And I've come to discover that the more I let go of my ideas, the more possibilities there are for learning. There is so much more to this life than what I can understand now. The Buddha Dharma is endless. So if I am in a monastery, I try my best to "just say yes" to the instructions people give me. This is because I know the Buddha Dharma is bigger than me, bigger than my life.

I think there is a really important distinction to be made between "nonthinking" or "wholeheartedly engaging the Way" and "being stupid." Nobody is telling me (or you) to be stupid.

Aoyama Roshi, my teacher at Nisodo, uses a useful metaphor to talk about the relationship between practice and study. In Buddhist practice imagine we are trying to play the piano. The historical Buddha and the various Buddhist masters are like great composers. They created beautiful symphonies and wrote those melodies down as sheet music. The Buddhist teachings—sutras, commentary, histories, all the myriad writings—are like sheet music. The sheet music tells us how and what to play. Without knowing how to read sheet music, it's nearly impossible to sit down at a piano and play music. So study is important, and thinking is important, and using your brain is important. But it's not the thing itself.

It's the same with driving a car. It's true that you can say you are a "driving master" only when you can drive without thinking. But to get to the point of "nonthinking" in driving, first you have to go to driver's ed, and then someone has to teach you how to drive. You have to learn the traffic rules. These traffic rules are not your idea. Someone else wrote these laws, but you've studied them and chosen to follow them. It's also important to know the kind of car you're driving, how many miles it has on it, and what kind of fuel it takes. After all this, it's safe to get in the car and drive without thinking.

So you need to know what kind of traffic school you're going to, what the teachers are qualified to teach, and what they're not. In the Soto school at least, the abbots of official monasteries are experts in monastery life—in rituals, form, and tradition. They've studied Dogen's writings and can give Dharma talks about Dogen's Shobogenzo and other important texts. They officiate ceremonies and can ordain people and give jukai. Those are kind of the basic qualifications. In my experience good teachers are also teachers of how to stand, how to sit, how to bow, and how to speak kindly and respectfully to people. I learn a lot by watching them move, talk, and work.

What no one is qualified to do, either in Japan or in America, is be in charge of my own personal, subjective experience. That is my space and my own territory. My likes, dislikes, fears, desires, and emotions are my own, and it's actually not the job of anyone else to change that—mostly because my personal, subjective experience is not the point of this practice. Practice is much more than that. In fact, I'm starting to like the word *training* a lot more than *practice* because instead of being a vague, quasi-spiritual term with no clearly agreed-upon definition, "training" implies, for me, that there is an exterior model I chose to follow.

Recently I was having a conversation with my Dharma sister about what we think are reasonable boundaries in spiritual communities. We agreed that within the confines of a monastery or institution, everyone has to follow the rules. If celibacy and head shaving are the rule, then so be it. If someone tells us to make tea for sixty people, that's what we'll do. If chanting is done in monotone, without dropping pitch, that's what we'll do.

But outside of the monastery, no one is in control of our bodies and our choices. No one has the right to tell me whether or not I can get married, or if I should shave my head, or where I can work or study, or what I should and shouldn't believe. An institution can and should control schedule and set standards on a daily level within its own walls, but in terms of big life choices and values—those are mine.

It's important to establish these boundaries, and I think I caused myself a lot of pain and suffering because I used to think that the solution to my problems was to get out of my intellect and to be in some nondualistic state of being all the time.

I became interested in Buddhism because meditation offered me peace of mind. I could sit and watch my breathing and not get caught up in obsessive thought processes. I needed that quiet, that space, that absence of thought. And I needed a practice to show me that I am not The Center of the Universe. I really used to believe that, and I was miserable. Noticing how I am a very small part of everything is a much healthier and honest way to live. The goal for me is to strike a balance between skepticism and trust, between independence and humility.

It's clear to me, though, that I should not be trying to dumb myself down. The Buddha said to give up lust, give up hatred, give up delusion, but he never told me to stop reading history books or to give up being smart.

BELL HOOKS, in her book *Teaching Critical Thinking*, writes about the importance of storytelling in creating community and healing from trauma. She quotes lyrics from a song in the traditional black church: "My soul looks back and wonders how I got over." Sometimes I don't know how I survived that time in the monastery, because in a certain sense that was the lowest I have ever been psychologically. I suspect that it was my bodhi mind that kept me alive, the mind that seeks awakening and truth. Throughout the suffering and upheaval, the part of me that wanted to know the truth stayed intact, and every time I moved or spoke toward that goal of knowing the truth, it got stronger. The truth of our words and speech lay their heads upon a greater truth that is beyond words, and it was this love of truth that made me leave my teacher, which helped me keep going, and which is writing and sharing this story.

Zen and the Art of Radiator Construction

Fall down seven times, get up eight.
—ZEN MAXIM

We're gonna need a montage.
—MONTAGE SONG, *SOUTH PARK*

I OFFICIALLY ENTERED NISODO in October of 2011, when I was twenty-five years old. I left Toshoji—Seido Suzuki Roshi's place—dressed in a traditional traveling monk's garb with a wide-brim hat, straw sandals, and my kimono and robe hiked up almost to my knees. One of the older monks helped me get dressed, although he didn't entirely remember how to do it, but half improvised from his recollection of his own experience. I carried a special box called a *kesagori* on my back, attached by a thick, gray cord to another pack lying against my chest. Because the monk had helped me somewhat haphazardly, the kesagori kept slipping off me.

I had to take the bullet train from Okayama to Nagoya dressed like this because Suzuki Roshi insisted I leave and arrive in traditional fashion. Monks don't actually travel this way anymore, and for my fellow train passengers, the sight of a young American woman in traditional Japanese monk clothes was about as unexpected as a pink, dancing elephant on a train, or as unexpected as...a young American woman in traditional Japanese monk clothes on a train. It was mortifying, and yet by this point in my Japan stay I was so used to bizarre things happening that I could sort of ignore the intense embarrassment and just sit in my seat until the train arrived at Nagoya.

That night in Nagoya I slept in a *ryokan*, a Japanese inn, and the next morning I had to put on the traditional traveling outfit again, complete with the precariously balanced two-box backpack contraption. By the time I'd taken everything off, slept, and woken up again, I had no idea how to put everything on for my actual arrival at Nisodo. There's a correct way to wear everything and tie everything up, and I had no idea how to do this, and when I tried to put the backpack contraption on, it kept falling down.

I called Suzuki Roshi in a panic. He ended up drawing me a very detailed and surprisingly skilled diagram of the outfit and pack and faxing it to me.

My training in Japanese Zen is exactly, perfectly described in this example: using a faxed diagram from a Zen master of an outfit almost nobody wears anymore, putting this on my body with no verbal instructions, and then wholeheartedly (or at least not 100 percent grumpily) embodying this outfit.

Most of my training in Japan was like this. The Japanese way of teaching and learning anything, whether it is art or making sushi or practicing Zen, is a lot of watching, eventual doing, being superconfused and yet not asking questions, having someone inevitably correct you, and then continuing on. When I began studying tea ceremony at Nisodo, which is a requirement for all nuns, I described it to my parents in a letter as a learning process—like being sat in front of a table spread with tools, wood, metal, and random objects and being told to build a radiator. You stare at the metal for a while (there with a blueprint that got faxed to you), and finally reach for the welder.

"No!" The teacher exclaims, "Use this first!"

She points at something, you're not really sure what it is, maybe a saw, and you pick it up. "Hold it like *this*," she corrects, and so you readjust. Then you sit dumbly for ten seconds, staring at the metal, at the unidentifiable tool in your hand, and since you're not quite sure what the tool is used for, you start to tentatively saw. "No! Do it like this!" and the teacher begins pantomiming something, but since she's not actually holding the tool herself, it's difficult to copy her movements exactly.

So you have fifteen minutes of this instruction once a month, and maybe in fifty years you'll have a radiator. Or some tea. That is basically Zen practice, which is why in Japan they say that "tea and Zen are one." I continue to practice tea to this day because I enjoy it and because it reminds me of Japan—but also because I think the kind of flexible, receptive mind it cultivates is so useful.

IT TOOK ME A LONG TIME to actually find Nisodo because I couldn't read the street signs, and I am embarrassed to say, I couldn't tell the difference between a traditional Japanese-style house and a temple. I literally wandered into strangers' front yards, thinking their beautiful, traditional villas were Zen convents. They weren't.

When I finally got to Nisodo, I walked through the front gate and down the pathway, which passed by the main Buddha hall. To my left I could see a giant metal bell, called a *bonsho*, suspended from the roof of a small pagoda. There was a sign hanging on the front door written in Japanese, which I couldn't read, and of course there was no doorbell.

I looked around but couldn't see anyone—but I could see a wooden mallet and a metal plaque for striking it against. I had been told that I was supposed to hit the plaque with the mallet three times because this is the traditional form of requesting to enter a monastery, so I picked up the wooden mallet in one hand and grabbed hold of the loop hanging from the plaque with the other. I hit the mallet into the plaque once and it made a loud, reverberating tock. I moved the mallet to strike again, and out of the corner of my eye I could see movement inside, and suddenly there was a very, very thin and tall nun at the door, making a face that looked like she was witnessing a small child being murdered.

"Don't…make sound!" She waved her hands in front of her face frantically, but it was too late because I had already sent the mallet crashing into the plaque a second time. Wasn't I supposed to be hitting this three times?

"No!" she hissed after the second strike, and this time I really got the message and stopped. I hung the mallet back up on the hook where it rested above the plaque, and I stood back to greet this nun who looked like she was about to explode.

"Everyone is sitting zazen!" she said.

I nodded in acquiescence and followed her inside to a small foyer beside the reception area. Directly in front of where I walked in, I could see an altar in an alcove in the wall with a golden statue of Kannon Bodhisattva (the bodhisattva of compassion) and a bright, energetic, perfectly symmetrical arrangement of flowers in a vase. The thin nun conversed quickly with an older, more serious-looking nun (if you can imagine) and then disappeared.

The older nun stared at me, neither frowning nor smiling, and said very quietly in Japanese, "Why did you come here?" She somehow had the ability to be simultaneously innocuous and utterly terrifying.

Thankfully I understood her Japanese and remembered how to use a few words. "To practice," I replied, not even remembering that this was the set, standard way new training monks are "greeted" at monasteries.

In Zen monasteries throughout Japan, there is always someone assigned to vet new trainees, and it's usually more extensive than this. At the bigger monasteries, monks have to wait outside for hours or days, sometimes in the snow, until they're let inside. But here they let me in right away. Most monasteries have a trial period called *tangaryo* where the new monks test their commitment and endurance over a weeklong period. They sit zazen all day, and they usually endure the most brutal criticism during this time, with older monks yelling at them and telling them they're worthless, sorry excuses for monks. These days people sometimes ask me about Nisodo's tangaryo period, and I say that tangaryo is not necessary because, at Nisodo, it's *always* tangaryo— every day is a test of commitment and endurance.

The thin nun reappeared with a blue bucket filled with hot water and a white towel. As she told me to take off my sandals, she dipped the white towel in the water, wrung it out, and placed it on the floor in front of me. She motioned for me to step on the towel, so I did, and to my embarrassment she wrapped the edges of the towel over my feet and wiped them down, cleaning off all the dirt and sweat.

The next few days were a blur.

Immediately I was sucked into the whirlwind tempo of events, work, and a million and a half rules, most of which I learned by allowing myself to be carried away in the unstoppable momentum of twenty-five nuns doing the same thing at the same time. Exactly ten minutes before (not more or less) the wakeup bell at 4 A.M., the nuns in my room arose silently and folded (but didn't put away) their futons on which they slept. Putting away futons or turning on lights before wakeup bell was forbidden, so everyone put on their kimono in the dark. Another thing I learned early on is that it is forbidden to show skin at any time, so I was required to always change under my clothes, even in the dark. When the wakeup bell rang we could put away our futons and go wash our faces and brush our teeth in the long sink outside the zendo. I learned on the first day (because I was reprimanded for not doing so) to cover my mouth with my free hand while I brushed my teeth, so as not to offend the mirror or person next to me with a view of my open mouth. To this day I still cover my mouth with my free hand when I brush my teeth, out of habit. Throughout each day it continued like this, rules upon rules.

THESE DAYS, every time I pick up a Buddhist magazine or book on "Buddhism in the West," there seems to be some discussion about whether or not Buddhism is a religion. These discussions are kind of strange to me because, at Nisodo and Toshoji and throughout Japan, Buddhism is *definitely* a religion. There is no debate. And Buddhism is also definitely a religion for the estimated five hundred million people who practice Buddhism throughout the world. In the morning at Nisodo, after zazen, we chanted for at least a half hour in front of a big altar in the Buddha hall. We would offer tea, cakes, and sweet water at the altars, and when the service was done we would go to another altar and chant there. Then we split up and got assigned work we didn't have a choice about. I'm not an anthropologist and I don't really know how to define religion, but you know how they say "if it walks like a duck, and swims like a duck, and quacks like a duck, it's probably a duck"? Yeah. For me, Zen Buddhism is definitely, 100 percent a duck—I mean, a *religion*. It's a religion!

WHEN I ARRIVED at Nisodo I'd already been practicing meditation for about seven years, and I'd already ordained and been living at a different Zen monastery. But Nisodo was a whole other level up of religiosity that I wasn't used to or prepared for, especially since my relationship to Buddhism at the time was about "my practice" (cultivating clarity, peace of mind, and compassion—or so I believed), not about offering fruit to a statue or rules about whether or not I could show skin while I changed clothing in the dark.

After a few weeks I met with the abbess, Shundo Aoyama Roshi, to ask her some questions. For the record, she's a very, very busy lady, and it was kind of her to take time out of her day to listen to a twenty-four-year-old American girl whine about atheism and forms.

"Americans are not interested in form," I told her bluntly. "So I'm not sure what I can learn here."

Sigh. Good ol' youthful arrogance.

But Aoyama Roshi was patient with me. She began by saying that little by little Westerners are becoming more interested in traditional forms, as evidenced by the increase in priests coming from the West to study in traditional monastic settings. Then she tried to say something the translator couldn't translate. I remember Aoyama Roshi looking a word up in the dictionary, then doing her best to pronounce it in English.

"Fundamentals?" she asked, trying out the word in English for the first time. "Fundamentals!" She seemed to enjoy saying the word. She explained that what I would learn at Nisodo were fundamentals, and that these could be applied anywhere, East or West.

"I don't believe in Buddha as a God," I continued. "So why are we making offerings to a statue of Buddha?"

Again she was patient with me. She affirmed what I already believed—that Buddha is not a God.

In Zen Buddhism at least, you can't say that you believe in Buddha the way people believe in Jesus or even faith in *kami*, the local Japanese deities. But at the same time, living itself is an act of faith—or maybe it's better to say, an act of trust. When you eat food you trust that your stomach is going to digest the food. You don't have to think about or will your stomach into digesting the food; you just trust that it will happen. Similarly, when you lie down to sleep at night, you trust that nothing bad will happen to you. You trust that you will fall asleep naturally, and wake up the next morning feeling refreshed. This is all faith in life, or faith in the universe.

In my experience, there is a lot of basic trust involved in Buddhist practice. First of all, I trust in my basic potential to *wake up*. This is a basic, fundamental trust that I touch in with every time I sit down on a meditation cushion. If I didn't trust that I have capacity and basic goodness, then I wouldn't be doing any of this. Even if, as a famous teacher once said, "Zazen is good for nothing," I still trust that it's a good thing to do. Figure that one out. I also trust—or suspect, or hope—that my teachers and my tradition know what they're talking about. This is a big one. The tradition of Buddhism has been around for a few thousand years, and it's included some of the most brilliant, dedicated religious figures throughout time all getting together to study, meditate, practice, and debate these issues. So...maybe it has something useful to say, you know? Maybe my limited twenty-nine years of existence on this planet can learn something from the Buddhist practice, which people have been dedicating their entire lives to developing for more than twenty-five hundred years.

Most historians trace the introduction of Buddhism to America (by which, sadly, they mean *white* America) to the Parliament of the World's Religions held in Chicago in 1893. One attendee, Paul Carus, was so impressed with Buddhism that he came to devote his intellectual work and writing to promoting this new, Asian religion. He wrote a book called *The Gospel of Buddha*, which rearticulated

Buddhism as a rational, humanistic religion that was compatible with science. When D.T. Suzuki first wrote about
Zen for an American audience, he rejected that Zen is a religion because it "eschews ritual" and spoke of Zen in terms
of "pure experience." His idea of Zen as "pure experience"
resonated with Western audiences. But the idea of a personal,
subjective experience is not something that inherently exists
in Japanese culture. The word for *experience, keiken,* is a
new word that was introduced in Japan in the Meiji period
(1888–1912) by translators who were already in dialogue
with Western philosophy. So it's pretty easy to argue that
the Buddhism we've inherited in the West is kind of a partial
picture, one that was tailor-made and redesigned for us.

Because of the way Buddhism was first introduced to
(white) America, people now seem most comfortable when
meditation is introduced as a technique with scientific background. Is there something inherently wrong with this? Not
really. I do see two small problems, though.

One is that appropriating meditation—taking it out of
a Buddhist religious context—ignores and overlooks what
Buddhism has been for thousands of years…which is a duck
(I mean *religion*). I'm not claiming I know what that duck
is exactly. Maybe there have been many different kinds of
ducks over the years, and maybe this duck is evolving and
becoming "Americanized," but it's a duck. And I think it's
a really, really, interesting duck that's worth studying and
not just throwing away.

The other problem is that supplanting "religion" with
"science" undercuts something basic and important about
explicit religious practice, which is the direct engagement

with and articulation of trust. Just because science explains how things work doesn't make our inherent trust in the workings of the universe go away. It doesn't make doubt and fear go away. Personally, I'm walking around with lots of unacknowledged doubt, fear, hope, faith, and trust all the time. Religious practice makes this explicit, providing us with a way to engage with this. When I bow to a statue of Buddha, I'm expressing my trust in something that is not me. I didn't design this universe. I receive life, and I trust that oxygen will be there and work out the way I need it to. So, thank you life, thank you oxygen, thank you body. I don't know how this is all working, but I'm happy it does.

Buddhism allows me to get in touch with my fundamental trust in the functioning of the universe, and this makes me feel less alone. If I read a study about how meditation lowers blood pressure, or how Tibetan monks have more gray matter in their brains, and then I decide to meditate because I want these benefits, that's still coming to meditation (and life) with a large amount of hope. I'm still trusting, or hoping, that meditation will lower blood pressure. The only difference is that I don't conceive of this as an explicitly religious trust. But it's still trust in something I cannot see or touch. I suspect that what brings people—especially Western atheist and agnostic meditators—back to the cushion again and again is that we need to be in touch with hope and trust somehow, even if we don't want to admit it and even if we don't want to call that religion. Because a world without hope is a world in which we feel depressed and alone.

And I, for one, didn't want to feel alone. So I continued to do practices I didn't fully understand; I continued changing clothes under my kimono; I continued covering my hand with my mouth when I brushed my teeth; I continued to (try to) listen to advice from people I respected; I continued to shave my head; I continued to sit down on a zafu every day and embody the posture of Shakyamuni Buddha. I continued sweeping the ground, going to tea class, going to lectures, asking some questions but mostly trying to listen and do.

The first night at Nisodo I cried myself to sleep, and I cried just about every day for the next year. By years two and three, I think I only cried once a week. I kept waiting for the time when I would be all cried out, but it never really came. The difficulty and suffering and cultural differences and inscrutable instructions kept piling on, but I stayed, and eventually I got better at handling the difficulty and understanding the instructions. And after about two years of watching and waiting and being yelled at and allowing myself to be corrected and learn from it, I was able to make a passable cup of tea.

The radiator still eludes me though.

8   Cutting Off Love

From lust comes grief; from lust comes fear.
Whoever is free from lust knows neither grief nor fear.
From craving comes grief; from craving comes fear.
Whoever is free from craving knows neither grief nor fear.
    —SHAKYAMUNI BUDDHA

THE FIRST THING WE LEARNED about at Nisodo was water.

In the sleep-dazed morning rush, when people were scolding us about not covering our mouths when we brushed our teeth, there was also a teaching about water. We learned just how much water to pour into the washing basin to wash our face, and we learned how to press the nozzle of the faucet up against the lip of the basin as the water poured out, so it didn't make a loud splashing sound. We learned how to rinse our toothbrush in a cup of water, to not waste, and we learned just how much water to use when washing the floor. We learned to pour used water onto plants outside. After paying attention to the quantity of water over and over again, we came to see that water is very precious, and that our seemingly tiny, everyday actions are actually very important. We came to see that there is no other place to practice than in this very moment, in this action, with this drop of water and this cleaning rag.

And we also came to see how little human beings actually need to survive.

THE LEADER OF THE WORK GROUP to which I was assigned was named Ejo-san. This was the woman who had wiped my feet with the towel when I first arrived. She was a former dancer, and she was very intense and strict. I remember one day I hung up the hand towels crookedly on the drying rack; she tore them down in a rage, pointed at the drying rack and screamed, "This is zazen! This is zazen!"

Now, separated by two thousand miles, this seems pretty funny, but the truth was she made me cry countless times. I was terrified of her, and I am embarrassed to say I actually wished on several occasions that she would die—or at least disappear—so she would stop yelling at me.

Sharing a room and working with her was like being trapped in a cage with a hungry tiger. And yet she also taught me many invaluable things. She taught me how to bow correctly, how to ring the bell, how to fold my *oryoki* cloths for the ritual meals faster and more beautifully, which language to use when speaking to seniors. She translated Aoyama's lectures for me countless times. In the first month at Nisodo I asked her, "Do you think it's okay for nuns to get married?" At that time I was technically still with Nate, although we were communicating only through letters by then.

She thought for a moment and then said something I would later understand was actually Aoyama Roshi's words: "I think if you want to be a wife and a mother, you can be a good wife and mother. You should do that. And if you want to be a nun, you can be a great nun. But it is too difficult to do both."

A few weeks later I ended the relationship with Nate. It was a long time coming, but living among other nuns, in a women's monastery, it seemed increasingly irrelevant and contradictory to have a boyfriend, even one halfway around the world. I also knew or suspected that I would be living in Japan for many more years, and he wanted me to come back and get married, which I didn't want to do. I just wanted to practice, to give myself over completely to the monastic container. He was sad but understood.

Sometimes people ask me why I chose to switch to a women's monastery, and I want to answer, "Why do women ever go to convents?"

The more things change, the more they stay the same.

IN THE CHAN TRADITION (as Zen is called in China), there are ten famous Ox-Herding Pictures. They describe various stages of training, progression on the Zen path. In the first stage, an ox herder is searching for an ox, which represents enlightenment. At this point, he has only a vague notion that the ox exists. Eventually he sees the ox's footprints; then he glimpses the ox. Next, he catches and tames the ox, then rides it home. In the eighth picture, he transcends both ox (enlightenment) and self (delusion). In the final stage, the ox herder returns to society to be with people. This final picture is often called "returning to the village." The ox herder no longer renounces the world on his solitary spiritual quest but shares his gifts with society.

Recently, I'm starting to think that there are seasons of the spiritual life. They are not as neat as the four seasons of Japan or the East Coast, but they are like the erratic summers of San Francisco, where cold fog rolls in only to be burned away by sun a week later. At times we chase the ox by entering a monastery, and at times we return to the market. And yet, even after we have returned home, there are times when we start to chase the ox again, running through the market in a frenzy, knocking over booths of food and dishware, hooves and whips and bridles everywhere.

When I was in Japan it was the season for chasing the ox, for leaving things behind. I have a memory of driving in the car through the Japanese countryside, when I was still at Toshoji. I was in the backseat, someone else was driving, and Seido Roshi was in the front. I think we were probably driving between the main monastery and his temple in the mountains. I leaned forward and asked him, "What's your favorite part about being a monk?"

That's a stupid question, by the way. I think that's kind of like asking someone, "What's your favorite part about being in the army?" What are they supposed to say? The smell of napalm in the morning? Actually that's kind of the answer he ended up giving me. His answer was, "Cutting off love."

"What?!!" I asked, surprised.

"Shaving your head means cutting off love. So monk means cutting off love." He was smiling and looked genuinely happy when he said this. For the record, this is the exact moment in time when I should have made a 180-degree turn and run in the opposite direction. Because I know now that it's impossible to cut off love—or at least when we cut off love we do this at the expense of cutting off or dampening other things as well. But I didn't run away. I kept walking straight into a bizarre kingdom.

In English the word *love* is kind of vague and can mean all sorts of things. Especially in a religious or Buddhist context, saying "love" can invoke ideas of compassion, kindness, and empathy, as well as the more attached kinds of love, like love for your parents, children, partner. But in Japanese, there is no ambiguity about *ai*, 愛, which means only attached love or affection. Ai can be love for your children, your husband, or your pet, but it's a different kind of love than, say, Buddha's feelings for all sentient beings, which would be *jihi*, 慈悲. *Jihi* translates as something closer to compassion or mercy. At Nisodo I heard the word *ai* used only in a negative way in Dharma talks. This kind of love is associated with attachment, obsession, and clinging, all of which the Buddha said cause suffering.

For many years I resisted this uncompromising party line of traditional Buddhist monasticism, the belief that *ai* should be done away with entirely if we are to find relief from suffering. When I first started meditating, I was convinced that my experiences in meditation of seeing the fluid nature of self were not, in a certain way, dissimilar from my experience of falling in love. When I was in love, I saw the parts of myself I always believed were "mine" quickly fall away—my boundaries, my ideas, even my ego, seemed to not be solid at all. And of course the joyful falling-in-love feeling felt something like a religious experience. So couldn't Dharma practice be like that? And even if they weren't exactly the same thing, couldn't they at least share space and make room for each other?

Unfortunately, the deeper I went into Asian traditions, the more I saw that, at least for monks and nuns, love is always viewed as a hindrance. I really didn't want to acknowledge this for a long time, kind of like how no one really believes they are going to die. ("We're all of the nature to die? That's not about me, right? That's about some other guy.") Japan, of course, is an anomaly, since most of the Buddhist clergy marry. Many historians trace the roots of this practice, at least in part, to Shinran (1173–1263), who founded the Pure Land sect of Buddhism. Shinran not only married a woman but also claimed this was a virtue, and claimed that he was "neither monk nor layman."

Over the next several hundreds of years, many Japanese monks (and to a lesser extent, nuns) married and had sex. Recently scholars have demonstrated that monks had been violating the precepts as far back as the Nara period (710–794), an act that was punishable by castration and other forms of public humiliation. In 1872 the Meiji-era government "decriminalized" marriage and meat eating for monks, leaving the prohibition up to the individual Buddhist sects to enforce. Whether this was to delegitimize the clergy or simply establish a separation between church and state is open to debate: the decriminalization happened at the same time as a larger persecution of Buddhism as well as a general societal shift toward modernization—including the Westernization and secularization of Buddhism. But regardless of the government's intent, the decriminalization had the effect of encouraging and giving government sanction to marriage for clergy. In recent years love and marriage have been rationalized in order to sanction temple inheritance, but Buddhism in Japan has yet to fully reconcile the paradox of married monks. Most Buddhist clergy in Japan hold celibacy as an ideal, even if they acknowledge it is an impossible one.

DOGEN LIVED AROUND THE SAME TIME AS SHINRAN and went in a different direction. I've scoured Dogen's writings for any positive view of love, and there's nothing. It's a desert. The most damning passage I've found about love (and there are a lot) in the Shobogenzo is from the "Gyoji" (Continuous Practice) chapter. This passage (in the Nishijima translation) keeps coming back to haunt me: "However we treasure the factors and circumstances [that we see] as self and others, they are impossible to hold onto; therefore, if we do not abandon loved ones, it may happen, in word and in deed, that loved ones abandon us. If we have compassion for loved ones, we should be compassionate to loved ones. To be compassionate to loved ones means to abandon loved ones."

What do we do with this? To be compassionate to loved ones means to abandon loved ones? *Really?!* Sometimes it seems incredible to me that we actually formed a religion around what this guy said. And yet, here we are.

After I eventually left Nisodo, people I told my story to would often ask me, "What about joy? What about love?" I don't want to give the impression that Zen practice is cold, bleak, and heartless, but on the other hand, joy and love were not big parts of my experience at Nisodo. So I usually answer that I cultivated strength and spaciousness with my own negative emotions, and from that place of space and strength, I can love and work better.

Renunciation is at the heart of monastic practice. For monks and nuns, renunciation is first physical and visual. We shave our heads, give up our birth names, beg for food, give up wearing the clothes we want in favor of Buddha's robe. This kind of renunciation is not limited to Buddhism.

Shaving the head, wearing religious clothing, and celibacy are tools and practices that have existed cross-culturally throughout time in religious communities. Catholic monks and nuns are celibate. Priests in many different religions wear special ceremonial clothing. Muslim men who complete the hajj customarily shave their heads.

Celibacy and renunciation are powerful practices, and I think especially for young women, when they are just learning to stand on their own two feet, it can be helpful to practice in a community with only women. When we don't have to think about how we look, about being sexy and beautiful, when we don't have to compete for male attention and approval, this opens up a tremendous psychic space. We are free to ask the scary questions: "Who am I when I am alone? Who am I when I am ugly? Who am I when I am nothing?" Of course there have always been and always will be women attracted to other women, and so women's communities aren't free from sexual desire, but a space without men is a different environment in so many ways.

The other daily acts of renunciation are transformative, no matter our gender, because they help us move beyond our small view of self. Usually in our busy, modern lives there is a list of things we need or want to do to be happy—or that we imagine will make us happy. We need a certain amount of sleep, a breakfast with enough protein and vitamins, coffee with cream and sugar, the right clothes, a commute that is not too long and full of traffic, good standing at a job that fulfills us; we need love and just the right amount of sex, but not too much. This is what I call the "human fulfillment checklist"—and it is impossible.

It's impossible because there is always something new and necessary that appears on the horizon. But if we are in a situation where these things are impossible—where the cream and sugar are not there, where the clothes that we feel beautiful in have been replaced by shapeless black robes—then we can begin to act from a place that is beyond our small sense of self, the tiny, bound conceptual cage of who we think we are. When we are stripped of the things we think we need—or, I should say, when we give these things up, gladly and willingly—for long enough, we find, paradoxically, that we have more time and energy for other people, that we have a greater capacity to meet challenging situations with flexibility and grace. But renunciation is a practice that needs to be continuously cultivated; it's not a one-time affair. This is why we continue to shave our heads when the hair grows back.

Aoyama Roshi once said that Buddhist training was like sailing in a boat that has a hole in it. The ocean water on the outside is the same water as the water pouring into the boat, only once the water is inside the boat, it will make the boat sink. So in Buddhist training we try to get the water out of the boat. The water inside the boat is selfishness, or attached love and craving, but when we get the water outside the boat and back into the ocean, it can make our boat sail faster. This is why there is so much attention paid to moving away from clinging and selfishness.

One of the most powerful ways to do this is celibacy, which is why monks and nuns across religious traditions have found it useful and important. Celibacy is a wonderful tool if it is something we want. For some people, being celibate helps them feel more spacious and more loving, not less. For other people, being celibate is deeply depressing and lonely, and for these people, to be forced into a strict form they don't want is harmful.

Each person practicing Buddhism will have a different way of navigating this balance between the spaciousness and freedom of renunciation and the pull of connectivity and love. To use a similar water metaphor, our relationship to the precepts and discipline is like a water wheel and water. If we are too far into the water—if we hold too fast to the rules, if we renounce too extremely, the wheel won't turn. However, if we are too far away from the water, the wheel also won't turn. We need to touch this stream of renunciation and have it move us, without running away from the water altogether.

Carl Bielefeldt wrote an essay called "Living with Dogen" in which he compared the unattractive parts of Dogen to the warts on the face of someone we're living with. How do we go about loving someone with warts? Some people may choose to ignore the warts and focus on the lovely bits, some choose to love their partner warts and all. Dogen's admonition to "cut off love" and "abandon loved ones" is a pretty big, smelly, oozing wart. But Dogen is actually not unique; he is in a long tradition of Buddhist teachers who admonish us to give up love, to give up our attachments completely. The language is quite clear and quite strong: cut, sever, drop off, uproot. And yet, in the West, we usually try to argue or apologize this kind of thing away—it's just an "Asian thing," maybe, or a thing of the past. We imagine we are beyond this, we have evolved, we see things from a more nuanced and absolute perspective.

For most modern Buddhists, at least those raised in developed countries where we are used to material comfort, if we want the water wheel to move, our task will probably be to move toward water, not away from it. To ignore the wisdom of past masters and teachers is arrogant, and it won't serve us in the end. And yet, each of us must express the truth—which is not *Buddhist truth*, but just truth—in a different way, just like different vases hold the same water in different forms. The same water exists in many kinds of vases. This is the wonderful paradox of engaging with tradition.

So: the first thing we learned about at Nisodo was water. We learned just how much to use, never wasting any. This is part of how we were taught to practice in every moment, in every square inch. Years later it is something I keep coming back to. I learned about life by learning how to pour water, how to use the right amount. In these small actions, I was able to step fully into my life. Something wonderful happens when we use only what we need and nothing more. When we pay close attention to each action, there is no place or time that is not important.

I never cut off love. I don't think this is possible, really. But time passed, things changed, and I left those men behind and in doing so stepped into my life.

9 # Enlightenment Is a
Male Fantasy

*Do not aspire to great realization. Great realization is
everyday tea and meals.*

—DOGEN ZENJI, SHOBOGENZO "GYOJI"

There are no symbols here to confuse you.

—JOHN CAGE

I WILL LET YOU IN on a big secret: I used to hate Zen.

In fact, sometimes I still don't really like Zen. I still sort of wish I practiced the kind of Buddhism where I live in the tropics, practice loving-kindness meditation all day, and eat rice from a banana leaf. This exists, right?

Nate introduced me to Zen, and this is probably why I hated it so much. Nate was a lovely, idealistic, over-intellectual type who could not cook or clean, and his mom bought his clothes. He loved the koan, the famous Zen story, of Nansen killing the cat. It goes like this: Some monks are arguing over a cat. The master, Nansen, holds up a cat and says to his monks, "If one of you can say a word, I'll spare the cat. If not, I will kill it." No one can say anything, and so he kills the cat. Later he tells this story to his disciple

Joshu, who then puts his sandals on his head. Nansen then says, "Ah, if you had been there, you could have spared the cat."

I hated this shit so much. I was coming to Buddhism with all of my suffering and anger and fear, and they give me a story about some sandals and a cat? This story always made me want the banana-leaf and loving-kindness meditation, thank you very much.

But of course eventually I met a real-life Zen master who talked about enlightenment and inspired me to ordain and try to get enlightened. I would sit in the zendo for hours, trying and trying to attain great realization, and maybe some things happened and I saw reality bend apart and open up, but this never solved the problem of my life.

When I was still practicing at Toshoji, a Japanese nun who had trained at Nisodo visited us for a month. This was before I had ever been to Nisodo, before I had any other reference for how to practice. The way this nun spoke made it sound like cleaning and administrative work is the end-all and be-all of Zen practice. My Dharma sister, an Australian nun who also lived at Toshoji at the time, joked, "She sounds like 'just do your work, concentrate on that and nothing more, enlightenment is a male fantasy.'"

The funny thing is, three years later my Dharma sister and I revisited this conversation, and it turned out we both more or less agreed. While it's not universally true that only men seek or want (or have "attained") enlightenment, Zen practice in Japan breaks down along gender lines in some very clear ways. For most of history, women have not had access to things like higher education, temple ownership, and authority codified through the traditional Dharma lineage. Zen nuns were prohibited from owning temples—and thus were cut off from the main source of income and authority for Buddhist clergy—until after World War II. Because of this lack of resources, nuns developed alternative strategies to survive—to find food and shelter as well as to practice. Most commonly, they learned and taught tea ceremony, flower arrangement, and Buddhist hymns to make a living.

Because of these historical and cultural specifics, Zen practice looks different for men and women. For those practicing in coed settings, like my Dharma sister and I had done, it became painfully clear that men's "spiritual work"—the Dharma talks, the *dokusan* (teaching in individual meetings), the earnest quests for enlightenment—were all made possible by women's work, by the women who cooked, cleaned, and organized the schedules of those men.

The scholar Paula Arai has demonstrated that in the face of societal inequality, instead of becoming resentful or complaining, Japanese Zen nuns attempt to convert their hardship and oppression into gratitude. Gratitude and full engagement with life become the main practice, instead of seeking an explicit kind of enlightenment on the cushion or a drastic overhaul of society. From a Western feminist perspective, this is a double-edged sword. Arai writes in *Women Living Zen*, that for nuns,

> practice is acting, being, sitting, sleeping. It is when these daily activities are done in accord with the Buddhist teachings that mundane actions become

practice. Displaying awareness of the reality of life, one nun [said], practice is "daily cleaning."

The first time I heard Aoyama Roshi give instructions for zazen she said, "Put your right foot on your left thigh, and your left foot on your right thigh. Straighten your back. Throw out any idea of Buddha or enlightenment."

So that's how I tried to practice. For the nuns at Nisodo, there was no time to pursue enlightenment. We threw it away, and what was left was the whole world in front of us.

AFTER THREE MONTHS or so of working in Ejo-san's group, I was reassigned to *tenzo ryo*, the group in charge of the kitchen and food preparation (*tenzo* means "cook" and *ryo* is "group"). We cleaned the kitchen, washed and chopped vegetables, kept inventory of the food, and prepared and stored smaller condiments like sesame salt, pickled plum, and dried seaweed.

One job that took up a substantial amount of time was the task of picking out the unpolished hulls from the polished white rice. The hulls are hard to chew and difficult to digest, and depending on the bag of rice and how well it has been milled, there could be anywhere from two to two hundred hulls floating around among the white rice. Sorting has to be done by hand, very carefully.

We would sit in *seiza* (kneeling, sitting on our feet) along a wooden table for hours, with a small handful of white rice poured onto a black tray, and try to find small stones and rice hulls. After the first half hour, my legs started to hurt and I got terribly bored. To pass the time and make the task more interesting, I would think about another famous Zen story.

In this one, the monk Xuefeng is working in the kitchen, picking sand out of the rice. His master asks him, "Are you sifting the sand and removing the rice, or sifting the rice and removing the sand?"

Xuefeng said, "I remove the sand and rice at the same time."

His teacher responds, "What will the great assembly eat then?" Xuefeng overturns the bowl. His teacher says, "One day you will study with someone else," meaning that Xuefeng understands a little bit but still has more work to do with another teacher.

On the one hand, there are no "wrong answers" in Zen practice, but there are answers in which people don't get to eat because you dumped out all the rice.*

So I was concentrating very hard on this koan about sand and rice and the great assembly, on relative and absolute, and I did not realize that because of my profound concentration on this koan I had completely failed to actually remove the hulls of rice. I had somehow misunderstood the instruction and wasn't properly identifying what was a hull and what was just an oddly shaped grain of rice. So all the rice hulls stayed in the bag. The next morning our porridge was full of them. During work we had to sort the rice all over again.

The next time around I didn't think about the koan of

---

*My writing-mentor friend, James Ford Roshi, who has studied and practiced with koans for over thirty years, would like me to point out that there are, in fact, correct answers to koans.

sand and rice, I just tried to actually take the hulls out of the white rice. This is also my experience of zazen practice. In the beginning I wanted some sort of enlightenment experience or understanding of buddha. I didn't understand how a sitting practice could literally be *just sitting*. I sat, and I tried and tried to get enlightened, and this got in the way of actually sitting.

But in a really important way zazen is actually just sitting. It's taking the inedible rice hulls out of the edible rice without making it some koan about the relative and absolute. If two Japanese nuns had that same exchange, I imagine it would go something like this:

> *Abbess*: "Are you sifting the sand and removing the rice, or sifting the rice and removing the sand?"
> *Nun in kitchen*: "You know, I'm just cooking dinner."
> *Abbess*: "Great, looking forward to it! Are we having miso soup or clear soup tonight?
> *[Brief exchange of cooking tips ensues, then both women carry on with work.]*

Maybe I don't get koans, but I do think that at the end of the day, actually cooking rice is more important than answering a koan about rice, because a koan about rice is answered in cooking rice well. Well, maybe I don't suck at koans. If any man wants to test my understanding of this koan, I challenge you to a rice-ball cook-off. First person to make a hundred rice balls wins the Dharma! Go!

Whenever I am asked to give zazen instructions, I give the same instructions I received: back straight, full or half lotus if you can, eyes open and looking down, hands in cosmic mudra. Take out any idea of Buddha or enlightenment and just do the posture. That's basically all the instruction I ever got, so that's all I say. I've tried to coerce teachers into giving me more instruction than that, but they never do. I was really frustrated with this for years.

And yet my understanding of zazen is that, at the fundamental level, you are just sitting there, embodying being a buddha. You're not doing anything other than sitting there. Of course when we come to zazen, we want all these things like peace of mind, concentration, tranquility, etc. And then the asshole teacher just tells you to sit with your back straight and get rid of any hope of enlightenment. Lame! I totally understand people's confusion.

If people ask me about counting breaths, I reply that some teachers will say that if you're really, really, really scatterbrained, then it's okay to count breaths or focus on your breathing for the first few minutes, but that Dogen was pretty adamant that you shouldn't count breaths. In fact, Dogen said it's better to have the "mind of a wily fox" than to count breaths. I tell people they can choose who they want to listen to. The exact quote from Dogen is this:

> In our zazen, it is of primary importance to sit in the correct posture. Then, regulate the breathing and calm down. In Hinayana, there are two elementary ways (of beginner's practice): one is to count the breaths, and the other is to contemplate the impurity (of the body). In other words, a practitioner of Hinayana regulates his breathing by counting the breaths. The practice of

the Buddha-ancestors, however, is completely different from the way of Hinayana. An ancestral teacher
has said, "It is better to have the mind of a wily fox
than to follow the way of Hinayana self-control."*

I've spent a lot of time worrying about not knowing
what to do in zazen and thinking I am not doing it "right."
I think everyone must go through this. My relationship with
zazen has of course changed over the years, and I don't worry
anymore about doing it "wrong" or "right," as long as I'm
doing it. So when I am talking to people with questions
about zazen, I am very aware that nothing I can say or do
is going to help them. I've had the same questions as they,
and nothing anyone told me helped at all. The only thing

*My parents are Theravadan Buddhists (Hi guys! I wrote a book!), and so
I feel an impulse to rationalize the term *hinayana*, to explain that the word
arose out of particular historical conditions and that all paths are valid and
not greater or lesser, as the word *hinayana* implies. Some Dogen apologists
like to argue that when Dogen says "hinayana," he is really referring to a
narrow mindset that can occur for all practitioners, regardless of the type of
Buddhism they practice. But personally, I think you just have to ignore when
Dogen says offensive things like this and move on, kind of like when your
teenage daughter says, "I hate you," or "I have to buy a pair of two-hundred-
dollar designer jeans because everyone else has one!" You just gotta be like,
"Sweetie, I love you, but no." And then you move on. You still love your
bratty teenage daughter, but you just don't take everything she says so seriously, because you acknowledge she's going through some hormonal things
and is probably insecure about her acne. That's how I relate to Dogen when
he gets into a "Hinayana scum" rant. Like, "I love you, but I'm just gonna
forget you said that, because clearly you're just grumpy and insecure about
not enough people signing up for the 'one true correct Buddha Way' that you
spent all that time and effort mastering in China." Dogen can just be a jerk.
That's fine. It's like Rousseau being racist. He can just be racist. We don't
have to blame it on "history."

that helped was sitting more zazen. The only good advice I ever got about zazen or Zen practice in general is: "It takes time." I never wanted to believe this, but I think it's the only advice that anyone gives that is actually true. You just have to sit for a long time, for many years, and then wisdom and trust develop.

There are no wise words that are going to help you because there is no substitute for doing it yourself. There's no teacher who can say anything that will be a substitute for your own time and effort. I believe this based on the very few years I have actually spent sitting zazen because, even in a few years, my relationship to zazen has changed so much. I can only imagine what it will be like thirty years down the road.

I think the only useful thing a teacher can do is to show someone that their life is their own life and their karma is their own karma, meaning that you're choosing how to live your life in every moment. I've never had a teacher "help" me in any other way than that. The most common thing that Aoyama Roshi told me when I went to her for advice about some problem was: "It's your life."

At first I took this as a really dismissive thing to say—it's your problem, not mine, deal with it yourself. In a way that's a part of what she's saying, but there's more. Another part of this teaching is that we *receive* life from the universe. Usually we think that we are in charge of our breathing and digestion, but this is actually happening without our consciousness. We receive our life, we borrow this life, and an infinite number of organisms support us in living. Once we notice this embeddedness, we feel compelled to act and face the world from a place of gratitude and responsibility—to work and study deeply, to practice in every moment, to smile, to own our own anger and jealousy, to not waste time. No one else can do this for us, and there is no time to do it but the present moment. That's a very powerful place to stand. We receive life from the universe—so it's not only our life, but it is our life because no one else can be responsible for it but us.

Kodo Sawaki, a Japanese Zen teacher known in English as "Homeless Kodo," infamously said, "You can't even share a fart with the next guy." I realize now that he's talking about zazen. It's your beautiful zazen practice, not mine. I can't sit cross-legged for you, or breathe for you. Yes, we're all connected to the great Universe and sharing the same air, but at the end of the day, it's just you staring at that wall, trying to decide if you want to count your breaths or not.

Dogen votes "not," by the way.

10   Die Standing

*Some people, when they have taken too much and have
been driven beyond the point of endurance, simply
crumple and give up. There are others, though they are not
many, who will for some reason always be unconquerable.
You meet them in time of war and also in time of peace.
They have an indomitable spirit and nothing, neither pain
nor torture nor threat of death, will cause them to give up.*

—ROALD DAHL

*In surveying the past, we find that transcendence of both
mundane and sacred and dying while either sitting or
standing have all depended entirely on the power of zazen.*

—DOGEN ZENJI, SHOBOGENZO "FUKANZAZENGI"

I TALK A BIG TALK SOMETIMES because I've found that the
way I talk to myself helps me walk a bigger walk. One of
the most important things I've learned in my life is how to
encourage myself, how to talk to myself in a way that helps
me not be overwhelmed by life's inevitable challenges. Then
this spills over into my daily interactions with people, and
they get the mistaken impression that I am some beautiful,
confident, realized human being.

My first summer at Nisodo all of my negative karma
ripened at once. That's the only way I can describe it. It was

as if every bad thing I had ever done in this lifetime and all previous lifetimes—all of my ancient, twisted karma, born through body, mouth, and mind—suddenly showed up at Nisodo in the form of hell on earth. In Buddhist cosmology, heaven and hell exist and are often portrayed in dramatic, angel- and demon-infested paintings, but most people these days think heaven and hell are just metaphors for states of mind. The human mind has the potential to create heaven and hell out of any situation. That being said, sometimes the situation skews it one way or the other.

I was working in tenzo ryo, sharing a room that was per-haps eight tatamis wide with five other nuns. When we opened our futons to lie down and sleep, our bodies were ten inches away from each other. Because we worked together and slept in the same room, we could never get away from each other, so if anyone had an interpersonal conflict, there was no way to have space. We also bathed with the same people in our room, so everyone could tell who had gained or lost weight or who was on their period. There was absolutely no privacy, so when we wanted to cry, we would go to the bathroom and cry as quietly as possible.

Tenzo ryo works the longest and hardest hours of any group in the monastery, and it's physically demanding because you're on your feet the whole day. It was about thirty-five degrees Celsius every day in the kitchen, which I believe in Fahrenheit is "really fucking hot." Most Zen monasteries throughout the world have three-month-long practice periods, but Nisodo, which used to be a certified high school before the war, runs on the Japanese academic calendar. So the period of time I was in the kitchen was not a three-month practice period but, rather, March to August. I ended up working in the kitchen every March to August for three years.

After I left Nisodo I joked with someone that if I ever wrote a book about my time in Japan, I would want it to be called *Everyone Is PMSing or in Menopause, It's Thirty-five Degrees, and I Woke Up at 4 A.M.*—because for many, many months, this was my reality. One of the younger Japanese nuns in my room was pretty mentally unstable and got into constant fights with an older Brazilian nun. At one point she trashed the Brazilian nun's desk—which was right next to my own—throwing her okesa, her nun's robe, on the ground, and the older nuns had to intervene and hold meetings with both of them. Eventually the younger nun ran away. A few days later her parents sent her back, and she had to bow in apology to everyone, full of shame. It was all very dramatic.

It's hard to describe how physically and emotionally taxing this period of my life was because so much of it was cumulative—a gradual, maddening increase of pressure like the Chinese torture method of dripping water onto a victim's head until they go crazy. Waking up at 4 A.M. to work ten hours in a thirty-five-degree kitchen with the same women you share a bedroom with and no days off sounds bad, but not *so bad*, right? Actually, a day or two or even a few weeks is not so bad. The hard part was doing it for months on end, as the temperature rose.

Tenzo ryo has the most work in the monastery, and very little rest time. I think we had about fifteen to twenty-five minutes of rest time in the morning, but even with this, I felt that I was always working. We were not allowed to drink water while working in the kitchen, for example, and if we were sick and missed work, then we had to put on full robes and okesa, go from room to room, bow, and apologize. This discouraged rest in a very big way. There was also a lot of added psychological pressure from older nuns to get everything perfect. The way Nisodo is structured is that the work groups themselves are run by novice nuns in training, with senior nuns making the big decisions and critiquing the outcome of day-to-day work. The senior nuns put a lot of pressure on the leader of tenzo ryo to make everything perfect, and this pressure would trickle down to us. During big, public events and ceremonies we would cook in the kitchen all day without breaks, eating a rushed meal of left-overs, and it was at the end of one of these days that I felt closer to death than I ever have. I was so tired—and I'm not sure tired is even the right word—that I felt like my internal organs and heart were slowing down, starting to switch off.

This lifestyle might have been tenable if I were in a good psychological condition, or if I had a sound grasp of Zen practice, neither of which was true at that point. I've struggled with depression since high school and started taking antidepressants in college. While I'm not a huge fan, I've spent my fair share of time in a therapist's office. I was pretty depressed when I went to Japan the first time, and about three months into my term in the kitchen everything came to a head.

I FELT PROFOUNDLY ALONE. There was one French nun and a few older Japanese nuns who were kind and helped me out from time to time, but they were in different work groups and very busy. For the most part I was with a tightly knit group of very stressed and overworked nuns who viewed me as a nuisance. One would yell at me every day for failing to do things like line vegetables up straight, or wring out the washing rags well enough. Because I could not understand Dharma talks in Japanese, I would spend days and even weeks without hearing a word in English about Buddhism or the Dharma. So from my perspective, "Zen practice" was just work, being reprimanded, and listening to hours of incomprehensible Japanese. Add to the mix being twenty-five years old with a biological predisposition for depression, and the result was pretty painful.

Pretty soon I was thinking about dying all the time.

I had had some suicidal thoughts in college, which had led to going on antidepressants, but nothing had ever been this bad, and I had never been so close to actually doing it. Every day I would wake up before dawn, when it would already be thirty degrees out, and listen to the cicadas whirring and whirring their mating call. Lying there, sticky with humid July sweat, ten inches away from the nun sleeping next to me, I would think about the best way of killing myself.

Would it be pills, or jumping off a platform into an oncoming bullet train? Did I have the courage and strength of will to stab myself? Is hara-kiri even a viable option? This was all in the five minutes I lay awake in bed, before my alarm went off. And then throughout the day, when the work never seemed to end, I would reimagine these scenarios.

I think any psychologist in their right mind would have diagnosed me with a depressive episode, but I think *overwhelm* or *exhaustion* are more appropriate words. I wanted to kill myself not because I hated myself but because I simply couldn't bear the idea of having to work anymore. Killing myself seemed like a more appealing option than continuing with that level of exhaustion and stress. In Japan there is a special word, *karoshi*, which means "death from overwork." It is a peculiar cultural phenomenon in which workers, usually salarymen working excessive overtime, will work themselves into a heart attack, whereupon they are found dead at their desks. I had read about karoshi before coming to Japan, as well as about the thousands of suicides a year by failed businessmen and overworked schoolchildren, but I never understood those stories or believed them until I spent time in an environment that put such a high premium on group conformity and output. It can feel like living in a vice.

At the time, I actually did reach out to an English-speaking psychiatrist who was working in Tokyo, whose phone number I found on the Internet. He insisted I send him $150 before he would talk to me about how much I wanted to kill myself, which I suppose on one level was the smart and sane professional move.

He listened to what I told him about exhaustion, being bullied, and wanting to kill myself, and he gave me the very smart and sane and professional advice that I should consider leaving the monastery. My response to this this was a nonnegotiable "no."

I brought up that I had been taking antidepressants since I was nineteen and felt like they were no longer working. I mentioned that I was concerned they were actually harming me and that I wanted to stop them. He advised against this and suggested I increase the dosage. After our hour-long,

$150 phone conversation, I never spoke to him again. I felt like I would literally rather die than follow the advice of a man who (a) required a huge payment before he would consider helping me stop wanting to kill myself, and (b) was not interested in considering my own personal authority. That was how my brain worked back then. In a strange, roundabout way, I guess he did help me, because I realized in order to avoid psychiatrists like him I would have to figure out a way, myself, to not want to kill myself.

So there was this French nun at Nisodo who was very kind and sympathetic to me. She wasn't always soft or gentle, but she was always kind. I remember telling her about how I wanted to die, and she said in her thick French accent, "Gesshin, you have to fight. It is like being on a crowded bus when dirty men keep trying to touch you. You have to push them off," and she made the motion like she was pushing people away.

You know how all the Buddhists (and really everyone who pays attention) say, "Everything changes"? Well, guess what, it's true! Impermanence means both the inevitable end of pleasure and joy and the death of loved ones, but it also means the mutability of negative psychological conditions. It means children growing up; it means the acquisition of new knowledge; it means grass growing toward the sun.

I once heard Aoyama Roshi say that human nature is like grass. When we are flattened, we want to grow up straight. And so the day came when I could no longer bear the voices in my head telling me to die. The French nun's advice stayed with me, and when thought came of wanting to die, I shoved it away. Like it was a pervert on a crowded train. It came back within minutes, and I shoved it away again. Eventually I became immersed with work and the thought didn't come back for several hours. But when it did, I shoved it away again. I repeated this for weeks. Little by little I began to feel stronger, until one day, I remember hearing a different voice in my head.

"Just go ahead and win," the thought said. "Just win everything."

So I decided to win. I decided to trust myself and deal with the full range of reality as it was happening in the here and now, approaching it with the confidence that I could bear the loneliness and fear that comes with being pressed up against the cold, hard wall of the universe with no protection. Part of this was that I stopped taking antidepressants.

Now, this is the point in which I feel obligated to say: Kids, don't try this at home. If you are experiencing exhaustion or suicidal thoughts, seek help. Don't stop taking your medication. What worked for me, and my unique experiences, worked for me because of my unique experiences. I don't think depression is a failure of strength of will. This is just my story. Everyone is different.

For me, part of deciding to win was realizing I needed to do more than just fight and endure; I needed to appreciate what was around me, to find beautiful things and things I loved doing to improve on. So I redirected my energy away from how difficult it was to live in such close quarters with volatile people and focused on my work. I focused on tea ceremony, which I was starting to love, and on learning to sing Buddhist hymns, which are called *goeka*. During my limited free time, I would go find an empty room and sing. After lights out I studied Japanese.

More than just working hard, I tried to put into practice what Aoyama Roshi was saying in her Dharma talks, which is that enlightenment cannot occur outside of the present moment, outside of the present actions of our daily life. Since our days are made up of actions like cooking, cleaning, studying, and speaking to people, the best way to manifest enlightenment is by giving full attention and care to all of these actions.

Once I gave up having an idea of how things should be and focused on my own two hands, it was as if the world opened up to me, because I could see how practice was everywhere. My practice was doing my best within that one tatami space I slept on, squished in between two nuns. It was doing my best to chop vegetables, and doing my best to sort rice. It was doing my best in the present moment, over and over again, no matter the situation, and not out of some aggressive, competitive drive but because the present moment was the material I had to work with.

IT'S DIFFICULT TO CONVEY the unique and important aspects of women's monastic training to a Western reader in a way that doesn't make it seem either boring, unfair, or unnecessarily painful (all of which it can be...but there's more to it than that—hence the difficulty in writing about it).

The piece I feel is most important to share about women's monastic practice in Japan is that there is no such thing as women's practice or women's Zen. What I mean is that while the exterior form of practice for women is slightly different from men's practice (we spend more time making and talking about tea, probably, and many of us have an obsessive interest in cats and snacks), it is the same Dharma practice. Or, as the second abbot of Eiheiji wrote: "Even though there are limitless forms of Buddha Dharma shown by buddhas and ancestors, they all are this one color of Buddha Dharma."

In the last chapter I joked that enlightenment is a male fantasy, but of course it's not only men that have fantasies of enlightenment; all humans have ideas and concepts that get in the way of experiencing life in the here and now. Enlightenment might be a male fantasy, and also there is no such thing as men and women's practice.

I spent the first year or two thinking that the practice at Nisodo was women's practice. There's a lot of attention paid to flowers, for example, and we were all required to study sewing and tea ceremony. In contrast to Toshoji, where I practiced before, there was a lot less emphasis on perfecting Dogen Zenji's monastic forms, and more emphasis on making beauty in our immediate surroundings. This led me to believe that there was some special way that women were practicing.

But I don't think this anymore, and I'm skeptical of any claims to a special, singular women's spirituality (just as I'm skeptical of a singular "women's" anything—including bathrooms. Whenever someone says "womanhood" to me I want to ask, "Which women are you talking about?"). If I am arranging flowers with my whole body and mind, without any idea of "woman" or even of "flowers," can this really be called a "woman's activity"? I have to believe that the mind being developed in this practice is the same mind that has been transmitted from the historical Buddha—that there is real congruence with the past. This is what Dogen Zenji meant when he wrote, "Pay no attention to male or female"—not that men and women don't exist, or that men and women are the same, but that practice and attainment is the same for everyone.

There's a narrative of women's Buddhism in some books I've read that women's highest spiritual potential is in the realm of relationships with family and children. Our biology is our destiny. While it's true that most women don't practice in a cave (though some do), and most women do practice by engaging with the world, it's also true that the vast majority of Japanese Zen nuns (and for that matter, most Buddhist nuns in Asia) engage with the world by remaining celibate and singularly concentrating on Zen practice in a temple. I don't think a life devoted to religious practice in community makes someone less of a woman.

A few people in America I've met expressed surprise when I told them that Nisodo, a women's monastery, was a lot harder than Toshoji, a coed monastery. I guess they assumed that women practicing together would be more light and friendly or something. But, for me, practicing with other nuns was the hardest thing I've ever done. I've met the strongest and least emotionally fragile women you can possibly imagine. There's a level of seriousness and concentration that I've yet to witness anywhere else, and most of the nuns have a very Japanese way of relating to emotional issues that makes me rethink all of my assumptions about women naturally being more emotional than men—well, except for rare instances of drama, which usually involved the younger nuns.

When I think of my time at Nisodo, I think of the Zen maxim "Die sitting, die standing" and how it perfectly encapsulates this attitude I'm talking about. Paula Arai explained, "Dogen used this classical Zen dictum in a widely chanted and studied text 'Fukanzazengi' [Universal Instructions for Zazen], to stress that practice means to do all activities with steady attention to reality here and now.... In Zen, although no one can verify how many people have actually succeeded in this, sitting and standing death postures are considered absolute proof of enlightenment."

I wouldn't be surprised if a few of the nuns I've met die standing, or in the zazen posture. It's how they live their life, and it's how I want to live mine too—fearlessly, and by fully engaging with each moment, with "steady attention to reality here and now." Whether or not I marry and have children, live with a family or in spiritual community, I want to do it with a straight back, on my own two feet. This is what "die sitting, die standing" means to me—not a morbid fixation with death but full commitment to all circumstances and moments, including death.

The first month I was at Nisodo, a senior nun told me, "People say the abbess is a man because she's strong, professional, and doesn't show her emotions. But remember that she's not a man. She's her own woman."

I think it's important to share representations of spiritual women who are their "own women." There are many ways of being a woman, and I want to tell the stories of women who die standing.

11   What Attainments?

When buddhas are truly buddhas they do not
necessarily notice that they are buddhas. However, they
are actualized buddhas, who go on actualizing buddhas.
   —DOGEN ZENJI, SHOBOGENZO "GENJOKOAN"

AOYAMA ROSHI ONCE SAID IN A DHARMA TALK that true selflessness is unaware of itself. True selflessness, she said, is like a person in a house up in the mountains lighting a lamp in their room; a traveler wandering through the valley below, lost and frightened in the dark, who then looks up and sees that light and feels comforted. The person lighting the lamp doesn't know someone else can see the light, doesn't know anyone feels comforted by it. That, she said, is true selflessness.

Lots of nuns helped me when I was at Nisodo. I mentioned being yelled at and overworked, and this is true, but there were half a dozen nuns who helped me develop practice with real traction. I talk about Aoyama Roshi a lot, and of course as the abbess she was influential, but in reality I think the most important people in a monastery are the senior monks and nuns, the people who are not in the highest positions of authority but who teach and lead the sangha in smaller ways. My tea teacher was always kind to me. Even though

I couldn't understand what she was saying, she was always patient with me. And the Buddhist philosophy professor liked me and always tried speaking English to me. I had three fabulous senior nuns in charge of training me at various points, who taught me everything I know about Zen ceremony, form, cooking, and right attitude. When I did my head monk ceremony in my third year, a senior nun named Hosai-san practiced with me every day for over a month, often after lights out, until I had memorized the complicated sequence and dialogue in Japanese. When I was working in the kitchen she would listen to me cry and then give me recipes.

And then there was Kito Sensei. She was ninety years old and lived alone in a small temple in Nagoya. Kito Sensei was the muse for Paula Arai's book *Women Living Zen*, the only book in English I know on the subject of nun's practice in Japan. She features prominently in Arai's writings, including her second book, *Bringing Zen Home*. But beyond that Kito Sensei is unknown outside the small circle of women practicing Zen in Aichi Prefecture.

Kito Sensei doesn't speak English and has never written a book. She doesn't have an advanced degree in Buddhist philosophy (I'm actually not even sure whether or not she went to college), and though she's incredibly respected and has had transmission for decades, she doesn't even really give Dharma talks. When she came to Nisodo, she would give small, intimate lectures about the life of Shakyamuni Buddha, but these classes usually took place in the dining hall, not the zendo or the formal classroom, often culminating with tea or a snack she'd brought.

The first time I met Kito Sensei was the first month or so I was practicing at Nisodo. I was having lots of problems with my ankles because of a sprain the previous summer that hadn't properly healed. At Nisodo everyone sits seiza for meals and lectures, and after a few weeks of this I ended up in the hospital. (Later I would see several Japanese women also end up in the hospital—so it's not just Westerners who have problems with daily seiza.) When I got back from the hospital, Ejo-san still made me work, and I was pretty distraught about being made to work with an injured foot. No one offered me a chair or any kind of emotional support. It was pretty bleak. One of the low points of my stay (dear God, other than the whole wanting to kill myself part) was when Ejo-san wouldn't let me go to the hospital a second time, or get acupuncture from a nun who offered it within the monastery.

"You've already been once," she said. "You don't need to go again."

I met Kito Sensei a few days after coming back from the hospital, when I was helping her run a sutra-copying class in the Buddha hall. At that time I couldn't walk properly, and sitting on the floor was quite painful, if not impossible. I must have looked physically uncomfortable because within thirty seconds of being introduced to her Kito Sensei asked me, "How are your legs?"

"They hurt," I said quite honestly. "I sprained my ankle a few months ago, and now they really hurt."

Kito Sensei was running the reception desk for the sutra-copying class, but she stood up immediately and walked straight out of the Buddha hall. She came back in five minutes, carrying some medicinal patches, the kind where you peel off the plastic and stick the patch to your skin.

"Here," she said. "Put these on your foot. It's for pain. And don't worry about sitting seiza. You can sit however you like here."

Over the years Kito Sensei's interactions with me were often like this. When I came to her room to say hello, she would slip me candy or even money, smile, then put one finger to her lips and go, "Sssshhh!"

But it wasn't just me she treated like this. I watched her interact with all of the training nuns, and she was the same way with all of them. Even the nuns who I thought were arrogant or mean she treated the same way, as if they were worthy and good and the only people in the entire universe who mattered.

Eventually, when I left Nisodo to study Japanese language at Nanzan University, sometimes Kito Sensei and I would go to dinner together in the city. She was the one nun from Nisodo who actually made an effort to see me after I left, and she was ninety years old! It was quite a funny experience scheduling a dinner date with a ninety-year-old Japanese nun, but we made it happen eventually, despite language barriers and our ineptitudes with cellphones and sticking to plans. She would pick me up in a cab and we would drive to this one restaurant she likes, and she would treat me to the kind of lavish dinner I experience only in Japan when some incredibly generous benefactor is picking up the tab.

Kito Sensei asked me lots of questions about school—about my classes, my roommates, even what I ate for breakfast every day. I tried to ask her questions about Buddhism, but she seemed way more interested in talking to me about how delicious our noodles were, about what my roommates and I did on the weekends, and how "great" my Japanese had gotten. The one time I tried to bring up Dogen she either didn't understand or was too uninterested to respond.

I've never heard Kito Sensei talk anything distinctly "Zen." I'm not even really sure that she sits zazen in her temple. I bet she still does morning chanting service, but I wouldn't be surprised if she doesn't do that anymore either. I think most of how she spends her time is chanting in people's houses, and then sitting down with them and having a conversation, where she looks them in the face and smiles, and is really present with them. But don't be fooled. Her whole life is Dharma, inside and out. Apparently it's just not something she really wants to talk to me about when we're eating awesome noodles.

WHEN I HEAR PEOPLE LAMENT how Buddhist women in Asia "don't show their attainments," I always feel a little conflicted. On the one hand, it's true that social inequality and discrimination exist in a very real way in Japan, and men are probably more likely to stand up proudly and claim their rightful place on the pulpit (or whatever). But on the other hand, I'm not sure what Kito Sensei "showing her attainments" would even look like. I'm pretty sure she is the attainment in and of itself; she is showing her attainment twenty-four hours a day, seven days a week, in every action she does, and so anyone can learn from her at any time. To ask her to "show her attainment" would be redundant.

Maybe it's that you can't ask a Buddha about "Buddhism." Maybe you can't ask a tree to describe wood, just like you can't expect a person lighting a lamp in their room, high up in the mountains, to know exactly who's watching down below in the valley, or to understand how the traveler in the valley, looking at that light, feels comforted and encouraged.

Is anything attained or not?

12   Don't Rush, Don't Quit, Don't Be Lazy

Shinkai Tanaka Roshi told me, "Understanding is not important; understanding is easy. The point is just to continue."

—TAIGEN LEIGHTON

BY MY THIRD YEAR AT NISODO, I felt like I was in my element. I could chant sutras "like a Japanese person," I felt engaged in my study of tea and Buddhist singing, and my Japanese had improved enough so that I could communicate and have good relationships with people. Every day I tried to view each activity as something important, even the things I didn't want to do—which was a lot. I saw my practice and view of Buddhism expand beyond the meditation hall to include all moments of life.

Rereading my letters home around that time, I am struck by how overzealous and optimistic I sound—about everything. I was trying desperately to find meaning in a bleak and difficult situation, and although I can tell now that much of my energy and optimism was forced, I can't help but admire the person who kept showing up, day after day, trying her best in a situation that was nearly impossible. Even though

I am a pretty intelligent and competent person, so much of the language and cultural cues were over my head.

That year I did my *hossenshiki* at Nisodo—my head monk ceremony. It's kind of a coming-of-age ceremony to mark the transition between novice and senior monk within a monastic community. Traditionally, the head monk is supposed to be as knowledgeable and realized as the abbot, but these days the role of head monk seems to fall on the most qualified person who hasn't yet done the ceremony. Both in Japan and in the West, it's one of the main qualifications for or steps along the way to Dharma transmission.

I did the ceremony in June, when I was back in the kitchen, working in tenzo ryo. In the months leading up to the ceremony, I was running the kitchen and rehearsing the ceremony after lights out. My memories of that time were of detoxifying bamboo by day, elbows deep in grimy water—and memorizing classical Japanese by night.

Nowadays in Japan, the format of the hossenshiki is a Dharma combat preceded and followed by several minutes of elaborately choreographed bowing. Ideally, the Dharma combat should demonstrate the head monk's understanding of the Dharma, but in Japan the exchange is usually a rehearsed set of phrases, not something spontaneous.

Aoyama Roshi felt it was really important to keep the traditional form of the Dharma combat, with several back-and-forth exchanges between the head monk and the questioner, instead of a spontaneous exchange that would be over in a few seconds. So she made me memorize most of my questions beforehand. However, for whatever reason, it was also decided that I would write and answer my own questions in

English. To this day I have never seen or heard of a hossen-shiki like this, with both classical and personal questions.

Each hossenshiki has a case, or koan, that acts as a sort of theme throughout the ceremony, and I chose to focus on a case called "Joshu Washes His Bowl." In this story a monk comes to the abbot Joshu and says, "I am new to the monastery, what can you teach me about Zen?"

Joshu asks, "Have you eaten breakfast?"

The monk says, "Yes."

Joshu replies, "Then wash your bowl."

I liked the simplicity of this story and thought it had a good correlation to my time in the monastery where I had so much struggle around everyday chores. I came up with three sets of question and answers about the Dharma and had someone translate them for Aoyama Roshi, hoping that she could verify my understanding. I don't remember exactly what I wrote in that first rough draft, but I do remember that Aoyama Roshi laughed and said that I had "so little understanding of Buddhism."

I was completely crushed. Naively, I had written down my spontaneous thoughts and feelings as answers to the questions, when in fact the traditional way to answer Dharma combat questions, at least in Japan, is actually through literary references. Aoyama Roshi sent me away to try again, with simple questions, and an admonition to study more.

After this experience I resolved to go to school and study as much about Zen Buddhism as I could.

LATER, AOYAMA ROSHI GAVE A DHARMA TALK addressing the case I chose. Because Dogen emphasized the unity of practice and enlightenment, she explained this means that we continue to practice even after we have attained realization, and even if we never attain realization. Practice and enlightenment are connected in the same way as the body and the mind, in the same way as our foot is connected to our leg: one leads and the other follows. "Washing the bowl" is stepping the front foot forward, continuing without hope or expectation of understanding, and then understanding follows, like our legs when we walk.

"When humans are hungry, we don't need to be told to eat," Aoyama Roshi said. "But to nourish our heart and mind we need to practice. And we need to continue practicing forever to satisfy this hunger. But we have to do it without expectation of enlightenment."

Over the years at Nisodo, the most common thing Aoyama emphasized to me was that practice takes time. I'm not sure if she says this to everyone or just specifically to me, because I was very young when I arrived at the monastery and had an idea that I should gain understanding and expertise very quickly. She often spoke about the "arrogance of youth," a prideful way of relating to the world, wanting results quickly and easily. In all fairness I'm sure that as an eighty-three-year-old Zen master she had a very different way of viewing the world than I did as a twenty-five-year-old beginner.

Yet despite her age, seniority, and realization, she always emphasized that she was just a beginner who was continually learning and discovering new things, and that all the great masters of the past were beginners. "The Buddha Way is endless," she was fond of saying in Dharma talks. "So we cannot say that there is one point in time that we, as finite, relative beings, understand the entirety of Buddha Dharma."

I remember one time I went to her room and started crying about what I was doing in Japan. She scribbled down on a piece of scrap paper: "Don't rush. Don't give up. Don't be lazy. Even Dogen Zenji took fourteen years."

ONCE WHEN I WAS IN OKAYAMA, I was invited to give a small talk at an intercultural event, along with the other foreign nuns from the monastery. In the question-and-answer session, someone asked, "What is the hardest thing about practice for you?"

One nun responded that she finds the cold the hardest part. Indeed, an old monastery in February is pretty damn cold. It was negative degrees that morning during chanting, causing my hands to stick to the metal bells. But when it came time for me to answer, I found myself saying that the hardest part about practice for me is just showing up for everything. The hardest part about practice for me is just continuing with practice. Whenever I go to a monastery or center, for the first few days or week, I am in a kind of "Dharma bliss," where everything is wonderful. No worries! I don't have to think about men (or...women?) or money or my future or anything extraneous. I can just sweep the floor silently and let my thoughts roll off like sloughing off dead skin. It's great. But eventually the glow wears off and I start skipping events. That 3 A.M. zazen session? I'm going to be sleeping through it anyway, so why not just sleep in my bed where I can be horizontal and fully utilize that sleeping time? It's the logical thing to do! Pretty soon I stop going to noon service because...

well, putting on my kimono is a drag, and my work isn't finished—and so on and so on. I spend an unnecessary amount
of time in my room, just avoiding others, avoiding practice.
Practicing in a monastic or residential environment always
shows me how selfish I am. It can be kind of embarrassing,
seeing myself this clearly. But I think this is the point of practice, to show us who we really are, not just how we imagine
ourselves to be. When we first start to understand who we
are, it is unpleasant, like listening to a recording of our own
voice. We think, "Is this what I really sound like?" But the
recorder isn't lying; it's we who are ignorant.

Once I watched a news segment in which I was interviewed about how to do zazen. It was painfully embarrassing
to watch myself on television. Why didn't anyone tell me
I slouch when I sit? Practicing with others is exactly like
this, like watching an awkward video of ourselves. Practice
shows us who we are. It's especially important to practice
with others, because alone, we can't see ourselves.

And so I am very grateful to community for showing me
who I am. Maybe the hardest thing about practice is seeing
myself, which is, of course, the whole of practice.

AFTER MONTHS OF INTENSE PREPARATION AND PRACTICE,
the day for my hossenshiki arrived. It was mid-June and
very, very hot in Nagoya. I had invited Seido Roshi and
about ten other monks and nuns from Toshoji to come to
Nisodo for the event. In honor of the occasion, Seido Roshi
donated a bunch of money and expensive noodles to Nisodo,
so we were planning a big banquet lunch after the ceremony.
I had given incense and presents to all of the teachers and

senior practitioners at Nisodo, and in return they gave me envelopes of money.

It was a huge event, and felt a lot like a wedding. The day before, in rehearsal, I was thoroughly stressed.

When we lined up in the Buddha hall to run through the ceremony one more time, I saw on the altar two large bouquets of flowers. The Buddha hall altar usually has flowers, but these stuck out to me because they were especially large arrangements unlike any I had seen in the temple before, filled with wild and fierce looking flowers, yellow and red spikes and hooks curling in on themselves. They didn't look Japanese at all.

"What are those flowers?" I asked the nun beside me.

"Oh, Ejo-san sent those for you today. She called to make sure the flowers arrived in time for your hossenshiki. She picked a Western style, for you!"

I received many gifts that day, but this gift of flowers from Ejo-san moved me the most. I hadn't spoken to her in about a year, since she'd returned to her family temple, but I still harbored painful memories of the suffering she inflicted upon me when she was in charge of my training, how she yelled at me and criticized me.

I recalled there were times when I actually wanted her dead, or at least gone, just so I could exist in peace—and I felt ashamed. I've never been as terrified of or as angry at a person as I was with her. And yet I knew that her harsh criticism, and the resilience I developed because of it, made me who I was that day. It made me someone who could do that ceremony, who could bow beautifully and scream the Dharma in classical Japanese as well as English.

I remember in my first month of training, when she taught me how to ring the big bell and prostrate between each ring, how every time I bowed she would criticize something, her voice laden with bitter resentment and disappointment.

"When you do your hossenshiki," she snapped, "everyone will watch you bow, so it must be done correctly. It must be beautiful."

And so she taught me how to bow beautifully. To this day I don't know if those flowers were a "congratulations" or an apology, just like I don't know if what I feel is gratitude or sadness.

13   No Precepts Observed, No Broken Precepts

The Ten Commandments are a warning from an
all-powerful, all-knowing God, eternally separate
from ourselves, not to do certain things or else He'll
kick our asses. The Buddhist precepts are reminders
to trust our own intuitive sense of right and wrong.

    —BRAD WARNER

If you observe precepts you know, that is not true
observation of precepts. When you observe the precepts
without trying to observe precepts, then that is true
observation of precepts.

    —SHUNRYU SUZUKI

IN THE SUMMER OF 2014, I met Brad Warner.

Actually—sorry—rewind.

In the summer of 2014, I told Aoyama Roshi that I wanted to take four months away to work on a Buddhist studies program in Kyoto. I had wanted to leave Nisodo so many times, but I waited until I didn't feel like I was "leaving" so much as moving forward to what I needed to do next.

My experience being head monk, my attempts to write a traditional Dharma combat in the Japanese style, and the painful realization of my own lack of knowledge about the Zen tradition and history of Buddhism in Japan pushed my desire to study Buddhism academically over the edge. My desire to learn Japanese, study in graduate school, and experience other things overrode my commitment to staying in the monastery, and I found a job teaching on a study-abroad program in Kyoto.

Aoyama Roshi had been encouraging me to study Japanese and go to school for a while, but since I had no money for tuition, I needed a job first. I left my status at Nisodo a question mark, telling them I would perhaps be back in a year. Then I went to America for a month in August, visited my parents, and spent ten days at Tassajara, the Zen monastery in California.

During the summer work season at Tassajara, residents and guest students work to support the guest season, a time when visitors come to do yoga and Zen retreats and enjoy the nature and hot springs of the surrounding area. I was placed in a general labor group and was assigned a different job every day, often outside cleaning up weeds or leaves, but sometimes in the kitchen or dining room. I shared a room with two laypeople. *Laypeople!* As a Buddhist nun trained in an environment where laypeople slept in separate bedrooms, I was shocked and scandalized at such blasphemy. What's more, there were no hangers to hang my *koromo* and kimono, my outer and inner robes. I remember being very offended by this.

And there were men. So many men! Tall men! Short men! Men who spoke my language and didn't think I was some strange, bald, bra-burning Martian. Or who did, but were fascinated by me regardless.

Everyone wanted to talk to me. Not just the men but the women too. At meals I was barraged with questions about Japan, the monastery, my life. Three weeks previously I had been at Nisodo, working in a kitchen, not speaking to anyone about anything other than bamboo and rice balls, and suddenly people wanted to know all about my thoughts and opinions and experiences. It was a little overwhelming.

The first or second day after I arrived, the director of Tassajara introduced me to Brad Warner, who wrote *Hardcore Zen* and a half dozen other books on Zen Buddhism. I'd never heard of him, but she told me that he'd lived and practiced in Japan for ten years and was the student of Gudo Nishijima Roshi, who translated the Shobogenzo into English.

I'd seen him in the zendo wearing a bright gold okesa and thought this was a little odd, considering he looked like an adolescent skateboarder, with shaggy hair and black, wide-rimmed glasses. But he was delightful to talk to. As someone who had practiced in Japan, I appreciated how he spoke humbly and with self-deprecation about his accomplishments. I thought he was funny and thoughtful, and he had an antiestablishment streak that I empathized with but couldn't quite embody.

I remember walking back to the student cabins with him one late afternoon. It was hot, the sun was beating down, and he was wearing cargo shorts, a graphic T-shirt, and sunglasses. After a week of Zen practice in California, I was in a heightened state of culture shock and was clinging to my tradition for safety and support, wearing my thin, blue summer kimono, a monk's work-robe top, and traditional Japanese sandals.

"This place is weird," I whispered to him conspiratorially as we passed the swimming pool. (A swimming pool! In a Zen monastery! Where was I?)

"Yeah?" he asked. "How so?"

"It's kind of like you have to be a layperson to be here. I don't know how to be a nun and practice like this. I can't just play bocce with laypeople, you know?" There was a bocce court near the dining room where I'd seen a lot of young people playing on their breaks, but I thought this wasn't appropriate behavior for a nun.

"Well, you could," he offered.

The thought hadn't occurred to me.

PLAYING BOCCE certainly wasn't breaking a precept, but my experience of training, especially with other women, was that proper bodily deportment helped me maintain the precepts. In Japanese, a word for *monastery* that gets used sometimes is *sorin* 僧林. The word combines the character for "monk" with the character for "forest." The implication is that a monastery is a place where everyone lives closely together and helps each other grow up straight, like trees in a forest, with nowhere really to go except up (morally and spiritually).

My experience in the monastery—and I'm sure I'm not unique—is that it's very, very easy to observe all the precepts in that kind of environment. If you're actually following the schedule and doing what you're told, it's basically impossible to break precepts because bad behavior is impossible: there's no sex (because everyone's too tired and/or another ordained person devoted to religious practice, and sex just isn't the point anyway), no alcohol (except for that one time we made pickled plums and then boiled down the excess to make rum—for the sake of not wasting), no drugs, and it's pretty hard to do things like lie because everyone can see everything, and it's hard to steal, because what would you even take?

My experience of this, though, was that all of this morally upright behavior was going on subconsciously. I was never aware of it. There was never a point when I thought, "Wow, I feel so calm and peaceful because I'm observing all of the precepts perfectly." I don't think it works that way.

There's a story that Aoyama Roshi would often tell to explain a good relationship to precepts. A monk goes to his master and says something like, "Master, you are so incredibly enlightened. How many precepts do you observe?"

The Master says, "I don't observe any precepts."

The monk is incredulous and says, "How is that possible?"

The Master replies, "I don't break any precepts."

"No precept observed, no precepts broken" is supposed to be the best attitude to take within the Zen tradition toward precepts. It's also the hardest because it's a slippery slope. Personally, it's easy for me to fall quickly into the "no precepts observed" side. There has to be a line drawn when I am actually observing precepts, where I am actively making an effort to do or not do certain things. Otherwise I'm just breaking precepts.

But what does "observing precepts" mean anyway?

For me, it inevitably begs the question, "What are the precepts?" Considering how many translations and interpretations there are of the precepts out there, I don't think it's an unreasonable question. The translation I received of the precepts before I received them was pretty straightforward. Don't kill. Don't steal. Don't drink. Don't get angry. None of this "intoxicate the mind of self or other" business. Just don't drink. That thing you're wanting to do? Just don't do it.

Even within this pretty straightforward, conservative translation of the precepts, there's a lot of room for questions, like what the hell is "not misusing sexuality?" What is "defiling the Three Treasures?" Before I took the precepts for the first time, I remember looking at this list and asking my teacher about the "alcohol" precept. I'd seen him drink alcohol after memorial services, and drinking is pretty common for Japanese monks, especially after ceremonies. I also knew I probably wouldn't be able to observe this one. You might remember that his solution was "don't drink too much."

Precepts in Zen are weird. They're weird because they exist as rules, but they are simultaneously invitations to explore for myself what I believe ethical behavior is on my own terms. But I like it that way.

In *Buddhism without Beliefs*, Stephen Batchelor writes about how the four noble truths are actually injunctions to act, not simply dogmas. He reminds us that the Buddha instructed us to "understand" suffering, "let go" of craving, "experience" the cessation of craving, and "cultivate" the eightfold noble path. The emphasis is on action, not belief. He uses an example from *Alice in Wonderland*:

There is a passage…in which Alice enters a room to find a bottle marked with the label "Drink Me." The label does not tell Alice what is inside the bottle but tells her what to do with it. When the Buddha presented his four truths, he first described what each referred to, then enjoined his listeners to act upon them. Once we grasp what he refers to by "anguish," we are enjoined to understand it—as though it bore the label "Understand Me." The truth of anguish becomes an injunction to act.

The same thing is true with the precepts.

For me, the precepts are not only guidelines but invitations. For a precept to be alive in my life and practice, I have to examine it again and again. I have to look at it constantly, and ask, "What is this?" And maybe this means I will "break" precepts in the process of coming to understand what they are. But then I can see and feel the repercussions and know for myself. Then the precepts become alive, and personal, and particular.

This is not to say that I think it's okay to go out on a coke-fueled killing spree just so I can understand what "do not kill" means. And an attitude of moderation ("don't drink too much") doesn't really work for the precepts about anger or killing. But I do think the precepts are most alive when they are being questioned, when they are in dialogue with lived experience. Making ethical choices based on external systems of value (societal norms, religious doctrine) seems to me like an insufficient way of going about things because it means I would be using someone else's definition of reality and someone else's experience instead of understanding for myself what is good and useful. I do think, though, that

I can use these external rules or guidelines as something that I am in dialogue with and that help me strengthen my own internal moral system—because it's the internal moral system, the one that operates regardless of external norms, that I want to cultivate and strengthen.

Even though the precepts are something we symbolically "receive" from an outside source, nothing is actually passed between student and teacher; nothing is transmitted. This is because we are already basic goodness and inherent enlightenment.

Personally, I view the precepts as pointing us back to where we already are, an external sign that says, "Look inside!" When I give up anger and clinging, when I stop bitching about other people, when I remember that, oh yeah, I don't want to have sexual relationships that make me feel confused and icky, there is a feeling of tremendous relief. This relief is the feeling, for me, of returning to what I already know to be true about myself.

I don't think there's some kind of magical "vow juice" that shoots out of the preceptor for us to mindlessly ingest. The only power the precepts have, the only power any of this practice has, is the power we give it, the meaning we make of it. This is why I have such a high tolerance for teachers, ceremonies, and ritual; they're inherently devoid of meaning until I create my own, through and with those external points of reference. It's an exchange between target and source language, between teacher and student, between external and internal. It's not entirely "mine," but it's also not something that's directly passed into me.

Of course, I could be wrong about the vow juice. Maybe

somebody really is squirting invisible, magical juice, but I doubt it.

LATER I WOULD VISIT BRAD IN LOS ANGELES, which, similarly to practicing at a monastery with a swimming pool and bocce court, was bizarre and mind-blowing. Actually, I'm not sure how much was Brad and how much was America in general. Being in America after so many years in the monastery felt like being on hallucinogens: everything was bright and swirling, and physical objects didn't behave how they were supposed to.

And it was really fun.

There was a coffee shop with animal heads on the wall and not one but two different coffee stations, one for fancy coffee and the other for *really, really* fancy coffee. The British guy pouring hot water over the coffee had a timer in one hand, making sure to pour at correctly timed intervals. There was the deep-dish pizza with sausage. There were tacos. There were palm trees and long streets filled with stores selling beautiful, expensive clothes. There was a movie. *I was in a movie!* When I got to Brad Warner's apartment, his friend was making a low-budget film in the living room, and some of the extras hadn't showed up, so they coerced me into acting. For the record, I really can't act. My life is about radical honesty, so pretending to be somebody else is hard. I remember the director, Pirooz Kaleyah, pulling me aside at one point and saying, "Gesshin, can I ask you to... act...more?"

So I sucked it up and "acted." I still haven't seen the movie though. It's called *Control Alt Delete*, and I'm pretty sure it exists—somewhere, either in real life or on the internet. I would appreciate a copy (I'm looking at you, Pirooz!).

I LOVE LOS ANGELES, AND I LOVE AMERICA.

But something about America—or maybe it's just lay life—makes me feel crazy. I get really overwhelmed by how many choices and options there are. I've never owned a smart phone (a friend pointed out to me that people don't call them "smart phones" anymore. Now they're just "phones"). All the new technology makes me batty. I just can't handle being able to carry around Facebook with me wherever I go and have it *ding* at me whenever someone likes a photo I posted six months ago. I hate being able to text. It makes me more obsessive than I naturally am, which is pretty obsessive.

I learned today that my generation is being dubbed the "face-down" generation because we spend all our time looking down at our phones. Apparently my friends all work in tech now and say things like, "My New Year's resolution is giving up chasing men. I mean, he 'likes' my stuff on Facebook, but what does that mean in real life?"

Well, I certainly don't know.

IT'S FAIRLY EASY FOR ME TO RATIONALIZE breaking precepts and to write chapters like this one on how precepts are just opportunities for exploration. When I write about things like celibacy, renunciation, and following the rules, no one wants to read that. Even I don't want to read that.

But when I write about how traditional Buddhism is crap and we can make everything up as we go along, people love it. Because…it's *America*! And we had the *fucking tea party*!

We dumped that tea in the fucking *BAY*! So take *THAT* Buddhism and your *RULES*! *I DUMP YOU IN THE BAY!*

I feel conflicted about this. I mean, yes, I want to understand truth for myself and all that good stuff, but I am skeptical of a view of Buddhism that places the individual self at the center and allows the individual self to act as the ruler by which everything else is measured (I mean "ruler" like the measuring tool, not a king). The individual self can understand things based only on its own, limited viewpoint, and this—all this—isn't about me. Using my own, small self as a ruler isn't the most accurate way to measure things, because I'll only ever be able to understand and evaluate things in terms of myself, in the same way that if you were using a standard ruler to measure the Empire State Building, you could measure only a foot at a time. Any measurement would just be in terms of a foot. When I'm using my self as the ruler, if something feels fun to me, I'll judge it as being ultimately good. If it feels bad to me, I'll evaluate it as ultimately bad. I can't see outside that, to something larger and more true. This is why it's tricky to evaluate Buddhist practice (and anything) based on whether you'll get personal enjoyment from it.

A lot of people I meet in America seem turned off by the idea of Buddhist practice because it's mostly hard. *If it doesn't make me happy, why should I do it?* And I've heard more than one person say, "If it's not fun, I don't want to do it."

This seems to be the pop consensus about Buddhism, at least in California, where I live. But "fun" has never been a part of my Zen practice. I wouldn't even go so far as to say that "enjoyment" figures in at all. That will sound depressing to 98 percent of people reading this, but I think about 2 percent will understand what I mean.

Enjoyment comes and goes. Fun comes and goes. The only thing I know how to do anymore is let go. Letting go is the only thing that feels truly and deeply good to me. Letting go is how I enjoy things.

I love America, and I think modern society is fun. I love my family, and walking through San Francisco, and playing around with clothes, and eating whatever I want, and intimacy and pleasure. And I want more and more of it. I want more connection and love and fun and intellectually stimulating conversation. I want all of it. I want all of it, but I can't have "all of it"—because I am insatiable. There's no end. And what is the "it" in "all of it?" There's no way to pin it down, to hold "it."

AFTER MY TIME IN AMERICA, despite meeting Brad Warner, eating tacos, and having my mind blown at the sight of a bocce court, part of me was really happy to go back to Japan. I knew I was going back to a situation where I wouldn't know anyone (again), and I didn't really know the language (again).

I appreciate teachers like Brad Warner, who encourage me to see things in less absolute terms; he makes me think that this practice is something I can do sincerely without completely sacrificing and changing myself.

But I also know I am an incurable literalist. I wish I could be one of those people who live "in the world but not of it," but I don't know how. I just know how to renounce things literally. I just know how to leave, to cross continents, to say goodbye, to cut people out, to shave my head, to wear weird clothes I don't really want to be wearing, to follow a schedule I didn't make, to study something I am not 100 percent enthusiastic about, just so that one day maybe somebody will learn something from it.

So I let go again. That's what it felt like flying back to Japan after a month in America: "I'm letting go again, and it feels good." Better than being in a movie. Better than all the tacos.

14   Yes (the Sex Chapter)

I think we have to do forbidden things—otherwise we
suffocate. But without feeling guilty and instead as an
announcement that we are free.

   —CLARICE LISPECTOR

I am not wrong: Wrong is not my name
My name is my own my own my own

   —JUNE JORDAN

IF THE DHARMA WERE AN OCEAN and my teachers were
buoys floating in that ocean, sometimes I would swim out
past them, to a place where I can't see the shore and have
no reference points.

Sometimes I am caught in a riptide dangerously close to
the rocks, and sometimes I am floating alone, staring up at
the sky.

In those times there is no teaching, there is no lesson,
there is just my small, human body and ocean and sky.

AFTER MY SHORT-LIVED MONTH OF FUN IN AMERICA,
I flew back to Japan to start a new job. I arrived in Kyoto a
few days before the Buddhist study-abroad program started
and met the director, a Greek man in his forties with a
shaved head and a goatee. There were ten students from

American universities in the program, and we stayed in a small, traditional Japanese inn for Buddhist pilgrims. The rooms were sparse—only a television and a low table, no chairs or sofas, and futons were stored in the closet.

But I was ecstatic. For the first time in nearly four years, I had a room to myself. I unpacked my things, put my computer on the table, and plugged it in. I bought ground coffee, a mug, and coffee filters, and put these on the table next to my computer and a small stack of books. I stood back and look at everything I'd collected, everything that was mine. No one could take it away or move it around or tell me when to use it or not. At night I turned on the heater just because I could.

When the students arrived the director and I picked them up at the airport. My head was shaved, and I wore a thin, green *samue*—a monk's work garment—because it was still warm during the day. The next day we had orientation, and I wore more formal robes and made tea for everyone, pouring a little at a time into each cup and then pouring in the opposite direction so that the strong tea at the bottom was distributed equally.

During the orientation, the director talked very briefly about rules. "Because this is a Buddhist studies program," he said, "the idea is to observe the Buddhist precepts within the inn. Let's say within the inn there's no drinking," he said. "But I can't stop you from drinking in general. It's Japan—you can walk around the corner and buy beer from a vending machine."

"I had no idea you could buy beer from a vending machine!" one guy exclaimed to me later. "I'm so glad he told us that!"

The students were loud and jet-lagged. They spent all their free time on computers and iPhones, listening to music and messaging friends.

In the first week I went to dinner with them and listened to their stories. Some of them meditated, but most of them said they didn't; there were philosophy majors, political science majors, and most of the religious studies majors weren't religious at all. But they were all interested in talking to me. They asked why I came to Japan, why I ordained, what the monastery was like, and what I'll do in the future.

"Will you always shave your head?"

"I'm not sure. I hope so."

"Can you get married?"

"I mean…technically, yes."

"What are you going to do now? Are you still a nun?"

"Yes, I'm still a nun."

"Even though you left the monastery?"

"Even though I left the monastery."

"You're cool," one of them said. He was a Jamaican guy who drank entire cartons of juice for breakfast and wore his headphones around his neck wherever he went.

"What?" I asked.

"You're cool," he repeated.

I laughed and laughed at this.

IN THE MORNINGS AND EVENINGS THERE WAS ZAZEN. The director put me in charge of organizing this, and I bought incense and a small singing bowl. Most of the students had never sat before, so I gave basic instructions about posture. Afterward, some of them asked me more questions.

"Can I count my breaths?"

"What about enlightenment?"

It was funny and weird to me to have people asking me questions. I found that when I talked to them, I was both enthusiastic and cynical at the same time; I oscillated between wanting to crush their dreams of spiritual attainment and wanting to cheer them on.

We settled into a nice rhythm. There was zazen in the morning, and during the week there were classes on Buddhist theory, history, Japanese culture and language. I sat in on the Japanese classes and sometimes ate lunch with the students in the cafeteria. The schedule was slow, and I had lots of free time to write, take walks, and do nothing. I wasn't really sure what my job was. The contract said I was supposed to act as a "liaison" between the students and the director, but the director seemed pretty casual and comfortable with the students too. I was technically the teaching assistant, but I didn't teach any classes and had no responsibilities besides disbursing the students' stipends every week.

After about a month I got restless.

THERE WAS ZAZEN IN THE MORNING and field trips on the weekend, but I had more time than I knew what to do with. I'd been wearing a samue until one day something snapped and I put on yoga pants, a T-shirt, and a cardigan I found at a free store.

When I walked downstairs, Taylor, the Jamaican guy, spotted me, and his eyes widened. "Gesshin? Are you...is that okay?" He'd never seen me in normal clothes before, and he assumed I was breaking a rule.

"I never made a vow to wear Japanese clothing my whole life," I snapped, more annoyed than I expected.

"So nuns can wear normal clothes?"

I rolled my eyes. "Technically I can do anything, since I'm an adult living in the free world."

Walking out on the street like this, I felt as if I were walking around naked. And, like being naked in public, it was both liberating and embarrassing, and I could feel the air press in on my ody like a vice. In the evening I changed back into Japanese work clothes and felt relieved.

But one day it was actually hot out, and I went to Japanese class wearing a black T-shirt—the one T-shirt I owned—which served as my pajamas in the summer. I'd bought a pair of black jeans, and on the weekend I wore the black T-shirt with them. The male students invited me out to a bar, and I actually went. It was a Western-style pub that sold overpriced drinks and had a live band playing, for some reason, lounge music. I sat on the high barstool and drank a margarita, chatting with the guys about Japan and Buddhism. The inn had a ten o'clock curfew, after which the front gate was locked, so we left the bar at 9:45 P.M. to get back in time.

It was a pretty tame, responsible night.

WEEKS PASSED and I continued with zazen, continued studying Japanese. I'd started a blog online where I wrote about practicing Buddhism in Japan, and it was really taking off. Complete strangers messaged me, telling me how much they loved my writing and asking me questions about Zen.

Often when I read these messages, I closed the screen

really fast and pretended I never saw them. To me, the messages were not from real people. I couldn't believe anyone would contact *me*, anyone would appreciate what *I* had to say, and so for the most part I ignored them—or tried to. The attention made me uncomfortable. I was so used to silence and following along with a group that I didn't know how to handle people listening to what I had to say.

In the evenings I went to dinner with the students at local restaurants. They were only seven or eight years younger than I, so it was not such a big age gap, and they were all so friendly and open I couldn't help but want to be friends with them. Over dinner we talked about meditation, Zen, politics, television shows, music, dating. Talking in English to people my age was like shooting up with a drug I'd been clean of for years; I would leave dinner feeling giddy and drunk, laughing over nothing.

One night a student, Nancy, knocked on my door to tell me she and some of the other students were going to the bars and did I want to come.

Nancy was tall, with a mane of curly blond hair, and she did yoga.

"What about curfew?" I asked.

"We'll figure something out," she said, smiling. "If we can't get back into the inn, there's all-night karaoke, or we can sleep in one of those outdoor cafes."

I frowned. "Really? That doesn't sound so good...."

"It's perfect," Nancy smiled. Her smile was wide and toothy, like Julia Roberts's, so big I think it might break her face. "It's perfect. Everything's perfect."

I couldn't say no to her. She reminded me of my friends in

college who were young and afraid of nothing—who could have fun anywhere.

"Then can I borrow a shirt?" I asked. "I only have this black one."

"Sure," she said. "But I just have T-shirts."

"That's fine. It's better than this thing." She came back in a few minutes with a yellow V-neck T-shirt. I put on jeans and the old sneakers I'd had since high school and headed into the night with Nancy and three other students

We walked to downtown Kyoto, which was so packed we could barely walk. Crowds of young people surged forward, laughing and talking boisterously, many of them already drunk. The lights from restaurants and pachinko parlors lit up the night.

"So this is what Kyoto looks like after ten o'clock," I murmured.

We went to two different bars, but the drinks were expensive, so we decided to go to a convenience store and buy a bottle of Vodka. Nancy bought cranberry juice and plastic cups, and we went down beside the river and drank next to the water. Along the banks there were groups of young people drinking and smoking, some of them playing guitar and singing. One of the students was smoking a cigarette, so I bummed one off him. Taylor looked mortified.

"Gesshin! No!" he yelled, but I laughed him off, and sat with a drink in one hand and a cigarette in the other, looking out at the black river reflecting light from the nearby restaurants.

A half hour later, when the bottle of vodka had been drunk, the group of us ventured back into the crowds. We walked down a street lined with trees, filled with strip clubs and bars, and finally decided on a bar and went inside. It was mostly Japanese customers, and they were all young, clustered around tables, talking and smoking a hookah. The group of us bought drinks and gathered around an empty table.

There was one other foreigner in the bar, a guy in his midthirties. He had dark brown hair and wore a crisp, white, collared shirt. He was a head and a half taller than I, which was impressive, since I'm already tall, but his shoes were black and shiny, which I was not so into. He told me that he was recently a CEO of a tech company.

"I did the money thing for a long time," he said. "But I got tired of it, so I sold all my possessions, and now I'm traveling around the world."

"You sold all your possessions," I tried to clarify. I was unconvinced.

"Yeah. I live out of a carry-on bag."

"That's cool. How do you do laundry?"

"Well…I try to wear things that dry easily, like this shirt. It's polyester."

"What happened to your house?"

"I sold it."

"You sold everything?"

"Except my guns."

"You have guns?" The thought was repulsive to me. "Why do you have guns?"

"Because guns are awesome."

"So what do you think about money?" I asked him, narrowing my eyes and saying the word like it was a dirty epithet.

"I think money is a tool," he said slowly and carefully. "It's not an end in and of itself, but it can be very useful to do good things. In the world I work in, it can be hard to do business without becoming an asshole. In a certain way you have to be an asshole to succeed, which is part of the reason why I am trying to get out, why I sold all my things and am traveling now."

"Okay," I said. "Fair enough."

I looked at him and his polo shirt, took in his attitude of easy confidence and his sheer physical size. I've always been wary of the kind of self-assuredness that goes hand and hand with being tall, American, white, and male. He reeked of privilege. It was as if he didn't have to try to be amazing at anything in order for everything to be handed to him. But oddly, he was so sure of himself that he came off as being humble. I felt calmed just by standing next to him.

He asked about the program I worked on, and I told him. "So, these are your students?" He smiled.

"No! Well…I mean, they're twenty-one years old, and I'm only twenty-eight, so it's not that big of a difference."

"So you're like the older sister who buys them porn."

"I guess."

"What were you doing before this?" he asked.

I took a big sip of my drink and looked away. I considered, very briefly, lying. What was I supposed to say? But honesty is ingrained in me, deeper than anything.

"I was in a Buddhist monastery," I said.

"Wow. For how long?"

I paused and considered again lying. But I was pretty drunk at this point and not feeling so shy, so the words tumbled out before I could stop them. "Four years, four and a half, something like that." His eyes widened, and he finally took in that my hair was about half a centimeter long.

"So are you like…a monk?"

"A monk, or a nun, yes."

He didn't seem so phased. "So in the four years you were in a monastery, were you celibate?"

I was drunk enough to not care about how forward he was being, and I answered the question frankly. "Yes," I said. "I didn't want to have sex. It wasn't what I was interested in doing."

"Can you have sex?"

"Excuse me?"

The guy actually blushed "I mean…sorry. What I mean is, academically, can nuns…have sex?

"Academically?"

"Yeah—you know…yeah, academically."

"Well," I said, raising my eyebrows. "Academically, and by that I think you mean historically, Buddhist nuns in Japan don't really have sex or get married, although male monks do. There's no vow of celibacy. But if you're asking if I'll have sex with you, the answer is you probably have only a five percent chance."

"Five percent chance, huh?" he said, nodding and gazing off into the distance with a thoughtful expression as if considering his odds. He turned back to me. "Then can I buy you a drink?"

I laughed and said yes.

When he returned, I downed the tequila he bought in one gulp and chased it with the rest of the beer I had. I spent the next twenty minutes talking to him, drinking, and smoking a hookah. I noticed the students had left, and Nancy appeared by my side to tell me they were all waiting outside to go home.

"I want to stay," I told her. "Is that okay? I'm sorry."

"Are you sure? Are you okay?"

"Yes, I'm fine. Can you get home okay?"

I realized, probably too late, that this was one of those "giving up my responsibilities as an authority figure" moments. In truth, I'd probably ceded that authority weeks ago, or maybe I never even tried to have it. Nancy actually looked happy with the situation and left with the other students to get late-night ramen.

The guy and I left soon and walked to the river.

The water was black, but the lights from nearby buildings were shining brightly. The banks of the river were still crowded with groups of young people. I sat on the grass, and he asked me question after question about my life. It felt like the first time I'd ever talked, and when he asked me if I was happy, I said yes without thinking.

After this, I wondered at how easily that answer came. At what point in my life did I become happy? I realized I took delight in saying it out loud and knowing that it was true.

It was getting late and I started to feel tired. "What time is it?" He looked at his watch.

"It's one A.M."

"My inn closed at ten," I told him. "I won't be able to get back inside, so I can't go home tonight. If you want to ever get to sleep tonight, we should probably go now."

"Are you asking to come home with me?"

"I guess so."

"Good." He smiled. "Then can I five percent kiss you?"

It was the first time in my whole life anyone had asked to kiss me. Usually whoever it is just does it, or I do it. I was so embarrassed I looked away.

"I don't think you have to ask that," I blurted out— because in my surprise and joy at being wanted, I forgot how much I value consent.

He turned my head back and kissed me.

I kissed him back.

It had been so long, but I remembered immediately what to do. It felt good. He lifted me up and suddenly I was sitting in his lap and his hands were around my waist, my tongue in his mouth. Behind me the river glistened black and gold. In a little while I stood, then took him by the hand and pulled him up. We walked together to the stairs leading up to street level.

"Four and a half years," he whistled. "That's a lot of pressure for me."

"You still have only a five percent chance," I said.

HIS ROOM WAS SMALL, the futon laid out on the tatami. There was a tiny kitchen—just a sink—and a bathroom. We got under the covers and I put my head on his shoulder, nuzzling his cheek with my nose. He wrapped his arms around me and kissed me. I pulled him closer until he was on top of me and I could feel the weight of his chest pressing on me, his tongue in my mouth. He slid his hands under my shirt, then pulled me up to a sitting position and lifted my shirt over my head. I took off his shirt.

Soon after, he asked, "Can I have sex with you?"

And I said, "Yes."

It was the second time that night he asked permission to touch me.

I stayed the night, and then the next day I went back briefly to the inn to pick up some things. The students were there in the common room, using their computers. One guy asked me how I got home.

"I found somewhere to sleep," I said.

"Where did you go?"

"I found somewhere to sleep."

Bobby, whose cigarette I'd bummed, looked up at me and smiled.

"You're my hero," he said.

I laughed.

One kid said, "Why is she your hero?"—but I was already out the door, already out into the street and back on the bus to that strange man's apartment.

I spent the night there again. I was drunk on his body. He took me and pushed into me, and when he did I was gone, completely gone. He brought me breakfast the next morning and asked me if I regretted sleeping with him.

"Yes," I said without hesitating.

But I didn't regret it because of anything related to vows. The regret was entirely beyond broken vows. Had I even broken a vow? Maybe? I don't know. Really, the regret was about sleeping with him specifically, how he was all the wrong things, how he embodied everything I despised. And yet, of course, that was why I'd done it.

"Was there one singular, traumatic event in your life that made you want to become a nun?" he asked.

"No," I said fiercely. "Why would there be? It was for good reasons."

Then I thought of Dave, dead a week after I slept in his bed. I remembered the weeks and months after his death, the confusion and disbelief, feeling somehow both numb and violently, physically ill. It was the closest I had ever come to insanity. "Okay, maybe there was a reason." I told him about Dave, but even as I told the story, it still seemed like a partial picture.

He told me about the former business partners whose life he had ruined. They had screwed him over on a business deal, so he kept a file on them and waited for the right time to "fuck them over." He told me how he missed his own mother's death because he was working. She was dying and he knew she had only a few days left, but he didn't visit her.

"She told me to stay and work," he tried to explain. "She forbade me to come visit her because she knew how important my work was. So she died without me saying goodbye."

Lying there, I wondered to myself: *Is he evil? Is this what evil looks like up close and personal?*

He took me in his arms and I let him do what he wanted. But before he did, he always asked me, "Do you want this?"

And each time I said "Yes."

Months later, even after I knew the worst side of him, after we realized we were just too different, after we'd called each other terrible names and said terrible things to each other—*Why did you pretend to try? Why couldn't we just let it be what it was?*—what I remember most fondly about him was this: I remember how good it felt to be asked, "Do you want this?"

And I remember how good it felt to say "Yes," and then over and over again, "Yes."

15   Great Doubt

The greater the doubt, the greater the enlightenment.

—ZEN SAYING

T<small>HE NEXT WEEKEND THE STUDENTS</small> in the Buddhist studies program and I went on field trip to Mount Hiei, the Tendai monastery where Dogen trained before going to China. Mount Hiei was like the Vatican or Harvard of medieval Japan: it's where all the most important Buddhist leaders trained and got educated. The temple complex itself is vast and incredibly beautiful, with dozens of separate worship halls, libraries, and living quarters.

One of the key features of Tendai Buddhism is "original enlightenment," the belief that humans are inherently enlightened. While Dogen was practicing at Mount Hiei, he was continuously plagued by the question, "If all humans are endowed with original enlightenment, why have all the buddhas throughout time needed to seek enlightenment and engage in practice?" He could never find anyone in Japan to answer this question, so he went to China, where he found a teacher who could.

I imagine that at this time, in the early thirteenth century, asking such a question of his teachers in the monastery would have been equivalent to something like asking a Sunday school teacher, "Could God microwave a burrito so hot he himself could not eat it?"

It probably wouldn't have been received very well by the powers that be.

The day before the field trip, I shaved my head and went back to wearing my monk clothes.

I walked around the beautiful, dimly lit temples of Mount Hiei feeling a deep sadness.

It was not a sadness from "breaking vows" or doubting myself, but doubting my tradition and my teachers.

Once we returned to the inn, I wrote this letter, in honor of Dogen's question:

Dear Old-Time Religion,

First, I want you to know that I think you're beautiful. I really do. There's nothing quite so beautiful to me as an old, quiet room, filled with the smell of incense. I think the old wood is beautiful, and the stone pathways are beautiful, and the high mountains where you build your churches and temples are beautiful. The *thangkas* and paintings are beautiful, and the altars—the gold candle holders, the offerings of flowers and fruit, the statues—it's all beautiful to me.

I need quiet, routine, concentration, and a certain level of seriousness in my life that I can't get anywhere else, so I'm drawn to you.

But I have to ask, is there anything there?

When you descend the steps to the inner sanctum, in the spaces where only certain monks can go, to wash important graves and keep the candles lit, is

Wisdom

WISDOM PUBLICATIONS

Please fill out and return this card if you would like to receive our catalogue and special offers. The postage is already paid!

NAME

ADDRESS

CITY / STATE / ZIP / COUNTRY

EMAIL

Sign up for our newsletter and special offers at wisdompubs.org

Wisdom Publications is a non-profit charitable organization.

there anything there at all other than old wood and old stone? In the gold lanterns and candleholders, in the flower arrangements, in the long hallways and shrines—what's inside them? Is there anything you can actually give me?

Are you actually interested in my questions?

Everyone tells me, "If you have great doubt, you will have great enlightenment," but do you really mean this?

Is it safe to ask questions only if I am also following along with the schedule? If I chose to define and live my life the way I want to, in a way that doesn't fit the prescribed form, are my questions still valid? If there's really no answer outside myself, why do I need you at all? Why shouldn't I just go out into the desert, into the forest, alone?

Are you really concerned with questions, or are you mostly concerned with preserving yourself? Is your most important priority just transmitting yourself? Is your most important priority actually to stay the same, to not change? Is your most important priority to cultivate and raise people who care primarily about preserving and transmitting your tradition? I've started reading the literature again that I was reading when I first became interested in Buddhism, at age nineteen. At that time in my life, before Buddhism, I was mostly interested in social justice.

And when I really looked into justice, when I really began examining how transformation of society is made possible, it became clear to me that love had to be a part of that transformation. Reading bell hooks helped. She was the first person I ever read who spoke about ending racial injustice and compassion in the same paragraph. She writes about the need for love to inform political change: "A culture of domination is anti-love. It requires violence to sustain itself. To choose love is to go against the prevailing values of the culture."

So I have to ask, without domination, could you survive? Without power? What if I were your equal in this? Could you still exist?

bell hooks writes, "My work in love has been to trust that intuitive self [which] kept saying that it would happen when the time was right. My work in love has been to trust that intuition knowledge."

What happens if I trust myself?

What if I chose not to follow?

If I trust myself, do you think you can teach me anything? Can you teach me something only if I inherently do not trust myself? Can you teach me something only if I hate myself, if I am afraid of myself and my own intuition? Is the transformation you promise contingent on my own self-effacement?

Because usually I think I can't do this alone. Usually I think I need help, I need community, I need guidance, I need a path, I need a curriculum, I need rules, I need shape, I need form. And that's what you offer me. Handrails. A container.

A way to stop listening to myself. A way to forget myself.

You tell me, "To study the Buddha Way is to study the self, to study the self is to forget the self, to forget the self is to be enlightened by ten thousand things."

What does that mean?

Love,

Gesshin

Can Nuns Get Married
(Academically)?

I agonized over the matter as best I could, and it took
an awfully long time for me to come to the conclusion
that the two paths of marriage and practice were not
compatible, and that I was seeking a world attainable
only by abandoning everything.
    —SHUNDO AOYAMA

THE MAN I MET AT THE BAR in Kyoto was the first but not
the last man to ask me if I "can have sex."

The further and further I gravitated away from the monastery, especially while wearing normal clothes, the more
I got this question from men. The wording seemed striking
to me because rather than asking, "Are you allowed to have
sex?," they chose to frame the question like an invitation
("Can you have sex?"). I would say this is offensive and
creepy—except I get it. If I were a man, I would want to
know if I could have sex with me too. It's a good question.

Women often asked me a slightly different question.
While I was at Nisodo, my mother sent me the novel *A*
Tale for the Time Being, by Ruth Ozeki, which is about Zen
nuns, the 2010 tsunami, and contemporary Japanese youth
culture. I wrote Ruth Ozeki a fan letter, and we had a brief

correspondence. She is a Zen priest and expressed interest in practicing in Japan but was hesitant because she is married. That was the first time I remember somebody asking me, "Do nuns get married in Japan?" On my study- abroad program, and later in America, lots of women would ask me, "Can you get married?"

Although sex, marriage, and permission to do those things are obviously a little different, for me they were very related questions. I realized that when people asked me "Can you have sex?" or "Can you get married?," sometimes the question was academic and sometimes it was personal. The academic version wanted to know something like, "What are the precepts for monastics in Japan? Are they different for men and women? What is the societal expectation? What is the history?" But then there were other people, like the man in the bar, who were asking both for the history and also if I personally wanted to have sex. With them. Now.

One question is easier to answer than the other. The word *nun* is the translation of the Japanese *niso*, 尼僧, which literally means "female monastic." It's an imperfect word because it brings to mind an image of cloistered Catholic nuns. But it's the most accurate term, and, importantly, it's the term Japanese nuns use to describe themselves when speaking in English. A gender-neutral term we also use is *obosan*, お坊さん, which is probably the word that gets translated into English as "priest." The precepts for male and female obosan in Soto Zen are the same. At the time of ordination, obosan take the sixteen bodhisattva precepts and shave their heads.

Hardly anyone in Japan interprets the precept about sex

to mean celibacy these days, especially since most monks marry. For hundreds of years in Japan, though, this wasn't the case. The precept about sexuality meant celibacy, and this was actually enforced by the government as well as the sangha. If a monk or nun had sex, they were breaking the law. There were so many infractions, though, that this law was repealed in 1873—along with the prohibition against eating meat. Male monastics responded by getting married in steadily increasing numbers. The same law was lifted for women a few years later, but nuns did not start marrying.

So the easy answer to the question of whether nuns can get married is yes. There is no law against nuns marrying, nor is there a precept against having sex. Nuns can do anything. Nuns are women, and human beings, and as adults living in the free world we "can" do anything within the limitations of the laws of physics. We can jaywalk. We can eat chocolate for breakfast. We can wear T-shirts. We can get married.

But most of us don't.

I don't personally know a single nun in Japan who's gotten married after she's ordained. Well I know *one* woman. Only one. She married a monk. So maybe there are a couple more like her out there. More frequently, married women will ordain after their children are grown, but even this is kind of rare.

The culture at Nisodo emphasized lifelong devoted practice. Nuns take pride in being nuns full-time—in not getting married, in shaving their heads, and in wearing monastic clothing even after they leave the monastery. Aoyama Roshi speaks pretty openly and explicitly about how "true monks and nuns" shouldn't get married. She believes that we are descendants of the historical Buddha, and that even though this is Mahayana Buddhism, we have an obligation to uphold the teachings and practices of the original sangha. Celibacy is a big part of this. For most nuns, there is no conception of "family time" versus "practice" or "monastery time." Being a nun is full-time, for life.

Other reasons for not marrying include practicality, personal ambition, and economics. Most of my teachers at Nisodo were nuns over the age of seventy who would have grown up at a time when women did not have opportunities to have careers or even necessarily pursue higher education. Becoming a nun provided another option. Aoyama Roshi was one of the first women ever to receive the equivalent of a master's degree from Komazawa University, the Soto Zen university. She was, of course, unmarried at the time. It's hard for me to imagine what Japanese man, in the 1950s, would have allowed his wife to get a master's degree in Buddhist studies instead of raising his children. Other nuns of that generation established missions and temples internationally—something that would be unthinkable had they had family obligations. By not marrying, nuns had the opportunity to educate themselves, travel in the world, and make their own choices. As the scholar Paula Arai wrote in a review of Richard Jaffe's book on clerical marriage, "Men escape domestic duties by marrying. Women escape domestic duties by taking monastic vows!"

I think it's probably also true that within traditional, religious Japanese culture, there is little conception of interpersonal, intimate relationships as a site of personal growth. I'm not sure there's even a concept of "personal growth"—that idea seems like something that originated in a Northern California meditation center. And I should know—I grew up in San Francisco with hippie, Buddhist parents. My parents have been together for more than thirty years and have always used their relationship as a way to better themselves, to become better communicators, to learn about their own faults and grow spiritually. They quote Rumi and Rilke to each other. A lot. This is the view of intimate relationships that I have inherited.

But I'm pretty sure that this kind of partnership didn't exist in Japan in the 1930s—and I don't know if it exists in Japan now. Seido Roshi, for example, grew up in a temple. His father wed his mother in an arranged marriage. When his father went to pick up his mother for the first time from the train station, he brought a cow with him for her to ride on. He was too poor to own a horse, so she had to ride a cow from the train station, up the mountain, to the temple. She always remembered that she had to ride a cow to the temple and would tell her kids that story. And she was unhappy in the marriage. When her husband wanted something, he would just ring a bell and she would come to him. I think this must have been a pretty standard marriage in Japan at the time, and not so much has changed since then. Actually, the birth rate in Japan is declining because fewer and fewer women are getting married, and they are having fewer children later.

So I'm conflicted. On the one hand, I do believe that intimate relationships are useful. I watched my parents grow and become better people through their marriage, and I've also been in love and been changed by that. And this is not prewar Japan. I continue to learn from and be pushed by wise and kind men.

On the other hand, it's clear to me that if I really want to learn something, it's better to just concentrate on that one thing. There is nothing for me quite like just doing Buddhism. Just living in a monastery. Just being a nun. There is no substitute for me emotionally and spiritually for that all-encompassing, all-consuming level of dedication and concentration. If I am thinking and worrying about a partner, I can't do that. I have to divide my time. And what if I don't want to divide my time? I'm also beginning to suspect that for me there is no one man and no possible intimate relationship that would be more fulfilling in the long run than studying the Buddha Dharma. Nothing compares.

I don't want to get married, and I probably won't—but not because I'm a nun. I don't want to get married because, frankly, I think it's an evil tool of white supremacist capitalist patriarchy that makes sense only if you want to protect your money and your stuff and your kids. If you don't have money and stuff and kids, there seems to be little point to it. And for right now at least, Buddhism is the most important thing in my life, and I can't really make space for anything else.

But love, on the other hand, love and affection, I have no control over. I can't choose whom I love, or when, or how. Delusions are inexhaustible, and I think until some chemist invents a medicine to suppress the production of oxytocin, I'm totally screwed.

So much for being academic about this.

17   Three Robes and One Bra

Although many laypeople have learned the Dharma
since ancient times, even those who were known as good
practitioners were no match for monks. Since monks
do not possess any property except for three robes and
one bowl, never worry about where to live, and are not
greedy for food and clothing, they will obtain benefit
as long as they devote themselves to learning the Way
according to their capacity. This is because being poor is
being intimate with the Way.

—DOGEN ZENJI, *SHOBOGENZO ZUIMONKI*

AFTER SLEEPING WITH A POSSIBLY (PROBABLY?) evil CEO who owned guns and did not visit his mother on her death-bed, I laid off the whole casual sex thing for a while. I didn't wear street clothes and stopped going out with the students. We went on field trips to famous temples throughout Japan, and I wore my kimono and traveling robes. I studied Japanese, wrote on my blog about Buddhism, and led zazen and chanting for the students. It was a very happy time, filled with new experiences. I was also profoundly confused about many things.

FALL CAME TO KYOTO and the evenings started to be cold. Kyoto in the fall is beautiful. The colors are brighter and more intense; the leaves turn deep red, and the sky in the evening is cloudy and pink. It was lovely to be out on the streets, dipping in and out of shops, but since it was my first time outside the monastic container in years, buying things was anxiety inducing. I had to make decisions like "do I buy toothpaste or milk this week?"—because I couldn't afford both. And then I would ruin my budget by buying a brownie instead.

Sometimes I would write about this on the internet, and kind readers would send me money through PayPal. "For toothpaste," the comments would say. Eventually I started to realize those donations were more for the readers than for me. Once I posted a photograph of a contemporary, art-deco *butsudan* (a kind of altar cabinet for a Buddha statue) I found in a high-end altar store in Kyoto with the caption, "Does somebody want to buy this for me?" I was joking, not expecting anyone to respond, but a reader at the San Francisco Zen Center actually sent me money. When I wrote him to say thank you, he responded, "I am having a challenging week and it is possible that donating to a worthy cause has made me feel better than any other thing I have done this week." This made me feel pretty guilty. How could I be a "worthy cause?" But I kept writing. Once I started I couldn't stop.

Dogen Zenji wrote, "Being poor is being intimate with the Way." All the religious folks speak so highly about poverty, so I wonder why it doesn't feel better. I suppose that's the whole point. The difficulty is the point.

I didn't grow up poor, so I guess you could say I had the privilege of choosing to be poor. I could have been having my parents pay my way through graduate school like most of my friends, but instead I was living in Japan, across from a construction site, in a seven-tatami room that smelled like old coffee and banana peels (my coffee and bananas, I admit). I hung out with twenty-year-olds for my job and tried to get them interested in Japanese Buddhism, though mostly I just ended up playing card games with them—and then stressing about how I couldn't afford milk.

Since I left the monastery I've been trying this weird experiment wherein I take "home leaving" and "poverty" as the foundation of my practice. Dogen stressed the importance of "home leaving" for monks and nuns as both a literal departure from one's family and a psychological endeavor to overcome attachment and conditioning. He also wrote about the importance of monks' being poor; he argues that these two practices are essential components of studying the Way. Even at times when I'm not following a monastic schedule, I try to make these the foundation of my practice along with shaving my head, wearing monastic clothing as much as possible, and sitting zazen every morning.

IN KYOTO I met a young Japanese guy who hated Zen priests. He associated them with demanding money from his family for funerals. Unfortunately, this is a common view of Zen priests in Japan.

"What is your *shugyo*?" he demanded angrily. *Shugyo* 修行 is the Japanese word that gets translated as "practice." I didn't really know how to answer. I should mention that he was pretty drunk at the time, and clearly angry about some other things—but I'd wished I'd had a good answer for him.

In a monastery, understanding what is "practice" is relatively easy. You wake up at the same time as everyone else and sit zazen together. You go to morning service, and then, if you have a liturgical service position like *ino* (chant leader) or *doan* (instrumentalist), you try your best to do a good job and not mess up the ceremony. Otherwise, you concentrate on just chanting.

Throughout the day, various jobs and situations arise, and you just focus on doing those activities single-mindedly, not putting too much of your own opinions and preferences into it. There's always a correct way, a form, of how to do things, so you can just concentrate on embodying that form correctly. And then, of course, there's the inevitable times when you get sad or mad or bored—and you can notice what's coming up and move on.

There's a phrase in Japanese, *igi soku buppo*, 威儀即仏法, which means "dignified behavior is the entirety of the Buddha Dharma." This phrase gets used a lot to express the importance of behaving correctly as priest and wearing robes. The idea is that being a buddha or studying Buddha Dharma is not something you believe in or think about or identify with, but something you *do*—and do repeatedly, moment by moment. Buddha Dharma is performed, not just understood intellectually. This is probably why, before I ordained, when I asked my teacher what the main difference between a monk and a layperson is, he told me that "a monk is someone who wears monk clothing." If you dress like a monk, you'll act like a monk. If you act like a monk, that's Buddha Dharma.

I remember having breakfast with my brother in San Francisco, and we were having a debate about whether or not people in Buddhism should "show their attainments." He was arguing yes. I voted no, and then added, "I think my only attainments are my clothes."

I still feel that way, sometimes.

This is all I have to show for myself, and for my practice: just these clothes.

In the monastery, if you'd asked me, "What is your shugyo?," I probably would have answered something like, "Igi soku buppo nari." But now I'm not so sure. I don't know if clothes are enough.

If practice is ritual enactment, what happens when I stop performing? What happens when I take off my clothes? (I mean this both metaphorically and literally.) I also have a hard time believing that practice is everything and everywhere. People sometimes say that practice is "single-mindedly doing what's right in front of you" or "just being aware." This implies that it doesn't really matter what you're doing, but how you do it. But if there's nothing I should or shouldn't be doing, then why talk about training at all? Where is the Buddhism?

The one thing I can say for certain about shugyo is that it is never-ending. In Japanese there are two different words that get pronounced *shugyo*. One *shugyo*, 修業, refers to learning or training in something, like a musical instrument. This kind of training is bound by temporality. This kind of training has a beginning and an end.

The other kind of *shugyo*, 修行, is understood to mean religious or spiritual training. This kind of training has no end. It started before I was born and will continue after I die. Viewing practice as something never-ending is encouraging to me. It means that there is no real way to fail at practice. I can always renew intention, renew my vows, start again. I can learn what kinds of situations make me happy and what kinds lead to suffering. I can relearn again and again that precepts are actually there to help me.

Within this view of practice as something never-ending, the most difficult and important part becomes renewing intention. Shunryu Suzuki Roshi wrote in *Zen Mind, Beginner's Mind*:

> Our spiritual way is not so idealistic. In some sense we should be idealistic; at least we should be interested in making bread which tastes and looks good! Actual practice is repeating over and over again until you find out how to become bread.

The practice just keeps going forever. This is why I like "clothes" as a good definition of practice. Since I have to put clothes on every morning, they are a way to renew intention. I put them on and remember, "This is what I'm doing; this is how I am living." I wear them into the world, and then people respond to me in a certain way, and I have to respond back.

And I know this isn't enough. Clothing isn't a good enough definition of practice. If monastic clothing is practice, what does that mean for laypeople practicing in America? What does that mean when I'm in the shower?

Some days I feel like my only attainments are my clothes, and if practice and enlightenment are really the same, that means my practice is putting on clothes too.

EVENTUALLY I CRACKED and did go shopping for clothes. Not robes, but *clothes*. Normal girl clothes. When I was at Nisodo my parents got rid of about 90 percent of the clothes I'd left in my room at their house—my skirts, shorts, blouses, and shoes. I guess they assumed I would never come back from Japan , and they were tired of my stuff.

When I moved to Kyoto, I brought only a samue, a kimono, robes, and one bra because Dogen said Buddhist monks should own only three robes and one bra (I'm pretty sure that's in the Shobogenzo somewhere).

I thought having no normal clothes wouldn't be so much of a big deal because I lived in Japan and I was a monk. But one week something snapped. I don't know why, but I got fed up with wearing traditional Japanese clothes and went shopping. I bought a red, knee-length skirt, tights, and a blue sweater.

SHOPPING IN JAPAN WAS A HILARIOUS NIGHTMARE. All of the women there are five feet tall, have no hips or breasts, and weigh fifty pounds less than I. The clothes tend to be "one size fits all," which is a cruel, cruel lie. The only reason I managed to fit into the skirt I bought was that it had an elastic waist. The popular style that was being sold in stores, at least in the elegant city of Kyoto, can be described as "Girly-Girl Prep." All the stores sold the same thing: knee-length skirts, dresses, thin, silky blouses, sweaters, and pearls. It was as if a yacht club got together with Hello Kitty, had a child, and made it five sizes too small for me.

But I actually really liked my skirt and sweater. The sweater was warm and soft, and when I wore it, it hugged my arms and made me happy. Most compellingly, I liked wearing it and looking like a normal person—being somewhat anonymous.

A skirt seems like crossing a line though, doesn't it? Pants and skirts are different. Pants are not so far away from a samue. They're functional. People need pants. People work in pants. Men and women both wear pants. But nobody needs a skirt. A skirt exists just to be pretty, and importantly, to look feminine. Wearing a skirt lets me perform "being a girl"—the kind of girl who wears skirts. In a certain way, the main point of wearing a skirt is so that when people look at you they think, "That skirt/girl is pretty. I'd like to talk to that skirt/girl."

Some days that's something I want. Some days it's not.

CLOTHES CHANGE HOW I FEEL ABOUT MYSELF. They affect the kinds of conversations I feel comfortable having, the kind of shops I'll go into, and the way I move in public. If I'm wearing monastic clothing, I'm not going to go into a pachinko parlor. It's just not going to happen. I'm not going to go to a bar. I'm less likely to break precepts. I probably won't lose my shit and curse someone out for cutting me in line. I'll probably be a little bit more patient and considerate. I'll be enacting a role.

Whenever I see a monk or nun in robes, I feel encouraged. It reminds me that there's another way of living. It makes me believe for a brief second that there is a possibility of freedom from my own obsessiveness and clinging. This encouragement comes just by looking at the clothes—it doesn't have to do with the merit of the person wearing them. The public role of a monk is an important role, and I want to perform that role when I can.

But I also think being a twenty-something wearing a skirt is a pretty important role too. After all, where would literature and art be without beautiful young women wearing dresses?

ONE EVENING I went out to dinner with some friends, and I wore jeans and my new sweater. I had really, really short hair—but I liked to think I looked sort of normal. The dinner was nice. Since I speak some Japanese , I chatted with the waiters—and there was a lot of bowing and the traditional saying the food was good. At one point they asked me to translate for a foreigner who'd wandered in with only American dollars and no yen.

There was more apologizing (for the food being late), and they gave us free matcha ice cream.

My first Japanese language teachers were monks, and they always taught me to speak very politely and respectfully. I think the style of Japanese I use is pretty formal and polite, and it feels nice to have pleasant, polite interactions with people .

When I was paying, one of the waiters approached me. "Excuse me," he said. "But are you a Buddhist monk?" He pointed to my head.

"I am!" I exclaimed. "I'm surprised you knew that."

When I got back to my table I said to my friend, "How did he know I'm a monk?"

"Probably because you are," she said.

"I could be a lesbian," I protested. "This could just be my cutting-edge style."

"No, I think it's pretty obvious you're a monk."

I'D LIKE TO THINK there's something about being a monk that doesn't have to do with clothes, something about me that pervades "home-leaving mendicant in search of the truth" regardless of what I'm wearing. I'd like to think that I can have my cake and eat it too: certainty that I am walking the Buddha Way and practicing the true Buddha Dharma, as well as enjoying the freedom to be young and do what I want and wear pretty things. I want freedom and pleasure and certainty and security—all at once.

I want buying a skirt to not be some irreversible turning point. I want to believe that there is some inner development happening that other people can pick up on—that what the Buddha taught is making me a good person, and that it helps other people, and they can see the practice working in me, and that even when I'm wearing normal clothes, people will still know I'm a monk—just like that waiter knew.

Though maybe it was just the bald thing.

Maybe it is the physical form after all.

Eat to Win

The original is unfaithful to the translation.
　—JORGE LOUIS BORGES

THE WEEK THE STUDY-ABROAD PROGRAM ENDED, we had a farewell dinner with our "Japanese buddies," the Japanese students who had signed up to be our friends and partners in intercultural exchange for the semester.

I didn't want to go to this party because (a) I was never assigned a buddy, since I was the teaching assistant, and (b) I am well aware how awkward Japanese parties are, especially the mandatory, organized-by-somebody-whose-job-it-is-to-organize-a-mandatory-party-above-the-cafeteria kind.

There is something about the way social interaction in Japan happens that seems simultaneously forced, formal, and too private; it's usually a huge room with lots of food, an exclusive group of people, organized games/speeches, and a group photo at the end. This is never a good recipe for making connection.

But my boss wanted me go to this one, so I went with the other students. When we arrived in the assigned room, we were immediately disheartened to see that the room was indeed made up to look like a middle-school dance. There were perhaps fifty chairs arranged in a huge circle for maybe twenty participants, and three tables filled with way more food than anyone could possibly eat. A tiny, white stereo stood in the corner playing Aretha Franklin *very* quietly.

After an obligatory organized group toast (with orange juice), the students and I filled our plates with french fries, fried chicken, and sandwiches. We sat down in a few of the fifty million empty chairs, and started eating. The woman in charge of the event immediately walked over and told us, in a bizarrely aggressive tone, "Don't forget to mingle with your Japanese buddies!"

Some of the kids were already complaining about how "awkward" this party was and how difficult it is to speak Japanese when you're really, really socially uncomfortable. I couldn't blame them, since I was thinking the same thing. But then some switch flipped in my brain. Without even trying, I tapped into a skill I have developed over the years at Toshoji and Nisodo to make meaning and enjoyment in even the most dire situations, like the characters in William Faulkner's *Absalom, Absalom!* who "had been walking backward slow for a year now so all they had left was not the will but just the ability, the grooved habit to endure." Okay, well, maybe not exactly like that.

What I have discovered through practicing Zen in Japan is that the best way to confront an unavoidable, difficult, and seemingly meaningless task is to get really, really into it. This means, in both monastic and awkward-party scenarios, that it works well to Take Everything Seriously and Get Competitive About All The Games.

This makes everything fun.

In "Genjokoan," Dogen Zenji writes, "In the practice-enlightenment of the Buddha Way, meeting one thing is mastering it; doing one practice is practicing completely." Another translation I've seen is "to get one Dharma is to penetrate one Dharma, and to meet one act is to perform one act."

Actually, this is one instance where I really think the literal Japanese is best. The Japanese is 遇一行修一行, which literally means "encounter one thing, practice one thing" or "encounter one practice, practice one practice." This is what's written on my rakusu case. It means, when you sweep the ground, sweep the ground. When you chop carrots, chop carrots. When you are at a party with unlimited buffet food, eat to win. When you are required to play "Find Somebody Who…" (where you have to walk around and find somebody who likes economics, or has an iPhone 6, etc.), get way too competitive about it even though it's not a competition and no one but you is actually writing names down. When you have to play two truths and a lie and are incredibly bad at lying because you are honest to a fault, go all out. For example, that might look like this:

(1) When I was in middle school, I broke my leg on a trampoline.
(2) I have an older half sister.
(3) I am a hippopotamus.

I really do think meaning can be found in all situations. People who've never been to Nisodo ask me, "Do you have much time for actual practice or is it mostly just physical work and Japanese cultural stuff?" But really, this question makes no sense me.

I was planning on going back to Nisodo for three weeks after the program ended, since I had never done my official exit ceremony. During the party I thought about how much I wasn't looking forward to it. For starters, I wasn't used to Nisodo anymore. I'd spent the last three months with the cushiest existence—waking up at a luxurious 7:00 A.M., eating the food I wanted, and sitting in chairs while I did it.

I knew that when I went back, I'd be waking up at 4:00, kneeling in seiza during classes, meals, and morning service, and working nonstop. And I'd have no control over my own time.

It was going to be a rough adjustment. I would also be the only Westerner there. It's hard being the only one of your ethnicity in any situation, and I think "foreignness" is especially pronounced in traditional settings that revolve around preserving and transmitting Japanese culture. There would be no English, as usual, and no one was going to translate for me. I knew the only way I was going to survive would be to get *really, really* into it.

I'm pretty sure this is what Dogen was talking about in "Instructions to the Cook" when he wrote, "This is the way to turn things while being turned by things.... Taking up a green vegetable, turn it into a sixteen-foot golden body; take a sixteen-foot golden body and turn it into a green vegetable leaf. This is a miraculous transformation—a work of Buddha that benefits sentient beings."

Did I really just compare Zen monastic training to making an awkward party fun? Well, maybe I did.

When I'm in the monastery, sometimes I want to run screaming for the hills. But sometimes it's the best party ever.

Either way, it's up to me.

In the whole world nothing is hidden.

THE STUDY-ABROAD PROGRAM ENDED and I returned to Nisodo for three weeks to officially say my goodbyes. As I mentioned, I'd left without doing the formal exiting ceremony, with the intention of coming back to practice—but three months in Kyoto had convinced me that it was time to move on. I knew I wanted to be on my own. Enough people had donated money to me on my blog, and I found out I had been awarded two large Buddhist scholarships, so I miraculously had enough money to pay for a year of college-level Japanese study.

My departure from Nisodo was anticlimactic, probably because there was no fitting ending to those three years; there is no ending ceremony that could do justice to that time. My friends stood on the porch, waving goodbye. Aoyama Roshi came out to shake my hand, a hilarious attempt to try out Western manners. I waved, and then walked away, rolling my suitcase behind me.

And then I was gone.

19 Being the Only Woman in the Room

Principal Skinner: When I look in my closet, I don't see male clothes or female clothes. They're all the same.

Edna Krabappel: Are you saying that men and women are identical?

Skinner: Oh, no, of course not! Women are unique in every way.

Lindsey Naegle: Now he's saying men and women aren't equal!

Skinner: No, no, no! It's the differences...of which there are none...that makes the sameness exceptional... Just tell me what to say!

—*THE SIMPSONS*

After I left Nisodo, I moved into a college dorm and began my new life as a mild-mannered, anonymous college student, just like everyone else. *Ha!* I was a twenty-nine-year-old, outspoken, world-weary, bald feminist who sometimes wore a black samue and sometimes a leather jacket, studying Japanese alongside nineteen- and twenty-year-olds who for the most part had never left Japan before.

I did not fit in. At all. Of course, I'm used to not fitting in, so it didn't bother me so much. I threw myself into studying Japanese. I went to class, studied until I fell asleep, then repeated. Eventually I did make friends. And I made my own way.

A FEW MONTHS INTO MY SECOND SEMESTER, I had to visit Zenkoji, the temple that had awarded me the international Buddhist studies scholarship, to pick up the money and participate in an awards ceremony.

My Japanese was okay and I understood Japanese Zen forms really well, but going to new temples was stressful for me, so I asked Seido Roshi if he would come along too. The visit was to be during Nehan Sesshin at Toshoji, which is a weeklong intensive period of zazen commemorating the death of the historical Buddha.

Seido Roshi met me at the Nagoya train station, and we finished the rest of the trek to Yokohama together. I remember that he hadn't shaved in about a week because of the sesshin, so he had a six-day beard. He was wearing a really ratty, patched-hole robe. The combined effect made him look like a crazed mountain hermit—which is a very unusual look for him, to say the least. As the abbot of an official training monastery, he usually makes a point to shave his head every five days.

When we got to Zenkoji, he kept apologizing to the hosts for having shown up without shaving his head, but of course no one really cared and no one criticized him—because, out of the two hundred or so people who came to that ceremony, he was the only monk who was actually sitting Nehan Sesshin. All the other monks lived in smaller family temples with their wives and children.

Seido Roshi proudly says to anyone who will listen that I don't want to practice at his monastery anymore because I don't like the "smell of men." That's definitely not true, and I definitely never said that! I can prove it because the phrase he uses in Japanese to say "smells like men" is idiomatic and not something I could have come up with on my own. Besides, I quite like men. Now that I'm out of the women's monastery, I seem to be seeking out men's company more and more.

I can talk to most men about things that most women are not interested in talking about. I like that men are usually taller than I. And I actually do like how men smell, which is often like some kind of men's deodorant (which is probably designed to make women think it smells good). So while I don't dislike the smell of men, Seido Roshi does kind of have a point. I really, really hate being the only woman in a room full of men—especially when all of those men are Japanese. Toshoji was mostly men when I ordained. There are a few women, but it's overwhelmingly a male, Japanese environment.

If you are a Buddhist nun in Japan, this kind of situation is statistically bound to happen. This is why practicing in a women's monastery was so important to me, and so meaningful. According to the Soto school website, 99 percent of ordained clergy are "monks," although I've also heard the statistic that 97 percent are monks and 3 percent are nuns. It's impossible to know exactly because the school doesn't keep records of sex/gender. But whether Soto Zen Buddhism in Japan comprises 99 or 97 percent men, what that means either way is there aren't a lot of women there, and it's inevitable that I end up in situations where I am the only woman.

Being the only woman in the room is not fun. It might sound fun—because, feminism! And men and women are equal! And...yeah—but it's not. Just trust me.

Being the only *Western* woman in a room of Japanese men is not fun either because, in my experience, men tend to treat me in one of the following ways. They either (a) completely ignore me, (b) flirt with me, or (c) put me on a ridiculous pedestal, gawking at my ability to use chopsticks correctly. I don't like any of those interactions. Never once has a Japanese man looked at me and asked me my thoughts about the developments of Buddhism in America, for example, or how I think Japanese culture supports monasticism, or what I think the role of the precepts is, or what I think about the Shobogenzo, or what I think about anything.

On the train to Yokohama I started to get nervous about the event, which, in addition to my receiving the actual award, was to include a particular kind of ceremony to honor the founders of the temple. I knew that I would be the only woman there, and that the people conducting the ceremony would all be Japanese men. I whined to my teacher. "I really don't want to go to this," I said. "I'll be the only woman there. It's just going to be Japanese men."

"Stand up straight," he told me.

That's pretty good advice for being a woman in a room full of men, I guess.

These kinds of ceremonies follow a set pattern that I knew all too well by now: You arrive at the front door and take off your shoes. Somebody leads you to the appropriate waiting room, because which room you wait in is determined by your status. There's always one or two private rooms for the important people and a big common room with bowls of snacks for the less important people. In both rooms, there are women serving tea. You drink your tea and talk to the people around you (or not), and then eventually it's time to change clothes for the ceremony, so you have to try not to feel embarrassed about stripping down to your kimono (essentially your undergarment) in a room full of men and putting on your koromo and okesa. Then you go do the ceremony. When the ceremony is done, you come back to the waiting room and change really, really fast into a slightly different outfit. And then everyone eats a bento dinner together, a Japanese style of eating in which delicacies like sushi and tempura are served in a box with many different compartments. No matter where you go in Japan, it's always the same bento, served with beer and green tea. And there's always some beautiful young woman in a kimono smiling and serving drinks.

Because I was the one receiving the award, I was in the "important person" room. I noticed the hosts were thoughtful enough to place the recipients of an international scholarship in the room of the temple with chairs. *Chairs!* Incredible.

When I entered the room, I was also overjoyed to discover that the other recipient of the award was a Bhutanese monk. Apparently there had been an influx of Japanese pilgrims to Bhutan lately, so this monk had been sent to Japan to study Japanese. We hit it off great. I've always been interested in that style of Buddhism, and I had traveled to Bhutan four years previously.

I told him how difficult it is to live in a college dormitory and keep on being a good nun. I sheepishly admitted that I wasn't always wearing the clothes.

He'd been a monk for more than twenty years, since he

was sixteen, and was wonderfully laid back and happy. "Our hearts will always change," he said, making the motion of something rising and falling, like a wave, "Sometimes we will have lots of faith and sometimes we won't. So the most important thing in Buddhism is just to continue."

I stood next to the Bhutanese monk during the ceremony, and at the time when everyone had to bow three times before the altar, he prostrated the Bhutanese way, putting his hands to his head, mouth, and heart to symbolize purifying body, speech, and mind. I liked bowing next to him—an American nun and a Bhutanese monk bowing in front of a Japanese altar.

After the ceremony there was indeed a big bento dinner. I was seated next to my new Bhutanese monk friend, which was great because, as expected, no one else wanted to talk to me except for the one drunk monk my age who came up and tried talking to me about how his teacher had married an American woman. Eventually I figured out that the two old monks across the table were the ones who had made the decision to select me for the scholarship—and I'd somehow managed to pass the whole afternoon not talking to them or saying thank you.

It's easy to become cynical in this kind of environment. When most of your interactions with men in a professional setting are them asking you if you're married or "How do you say 'I love you' in English?" When the only other women in the room are serving tea and sake, it's easy to become hopeless about the state of gender relations and the possibility of women ever being treated equally. But these men had given me scholarship money, and I was grateful. So I got up my courage, made eye contact with the old monk across the table, and bowed.

"Thank you very much for the opportunity," I said in Japanese. "Studying kanji is very difficult, but I'll do my best."

Then the old monk did something I wasn't expecting. He smiled very brightly and looked me straight in the eye. Then he said to me in perfect English, "I am expecting your translation of the Shobogenzo."

I laughed nervously. On my application for the scholarship I had said I was interested in studying Japanese to do translation work on things like the Shobogenzo, but this felt like he was saying, "I expect you to go to the moon." Reading the Shobogenzo is near impossible, even for Japanese people. The Shobogenzo is translated in groups by bilingual experts who have been studying Dogen and Zen for decades.

"Please wait a little," I said, trying to shake off his compliment. The monk stopped smiling.

"I'm quite serious," he said. "We are all expecting your translation. We could choose only two people for this scholarship." Then he smiled again. "Do your best! I am waiting for you!"

I was very touched.

SOMETIMES I NEVER KNEW WHY I WAS IN JAPAN, or why I was doing what I was doing. I had to spend a lot of time with people who didn't look like me, who didn't understand me, who don't speak my language. Sometimes I had to be in rooms filled with much older men who were confused and slightly pissed off by the presence of a young, foreign (pretty?) nun in their midst.

But every so often, one of those men would actually see me for who I am and would tell me he expects me to go to the moon.

20   # The Man with the
      # Heart Sutra Tattoo

If there is only one thing in my life that I am proud of,
it's that I have never been a kept woman.

—MARILYN MONROE

JOSH CHAN: I'm fine with being alone. Listen, I love
*   solitaire, I love Solo cups, I love playing Uno...*
ALEX: That game's for two people.

—*CRAZY EX-GIRLFRIEND*

WHILE I WAS IN SCHOOL I WROTE a Facebook post that said, "Both the Buddha and Dogen had extremely powerful and wealthy benefactors, and Zen priests in Japan make thousands of dollars on funeral services, so why do I still feel guilty about making money?"

I don't remember exactly why I wrote this, although it probably had to do with receiving a small donation. By that point I had several hundred, if not thousands, of people reading my blog, and periodically readers would send me money electronically. I made just enough to buy food and other necessities.

But the Zen purist in me had a lot of baggage around money. Later that day, after posting about my guilt around

earning money, I received a one-hundred-dollar PayPal donation from a man at the San Francisco Zen Center. It was
the same man who had sent me money back when I was
living in Kyoto to buy the fancy Buddha altar. This time
the note said, "Something to practice with." One month
later, in September, he sent me money again. The note said,
"Because I will be away and won't be able to donate in time
for Christmas."

I AM VERY CAREFUL ABOUT MEN AND MONEY.

One of the fortunate/unfortunate problems with being a
young(ish) attractive woman is that men want to buy me
things. This is fortunate because I actually need money, and
it is unfortunate because accepting "because I'm pretty"
money is problematic and leads to power imbalances.

I know that my writing is good and people are inspired by
my practice (for whatever reason), but also I have a picture of
my face on my blog—and a lot of my readers and donors are
men. Things are complicated because of my ordination status and the fact that I am attempting to go through life as a
mendicant, relying on support from others, or through work
that I consider Dharma related. So I do need the support
that I ask for and receive. I don't actually have the luxury of
saying no to half the population. Yet I was a feminist before
I was a Buddhist nun, and I hate when men want to buy me
things. Relying on men makes me uncomfortable. How is it
possible to practice self-sufficiency and healthy boundaries,
especially with men, when I am literally begging for money?

In many ways, contemporary feminism and traditional
Buddhism diverge here. The mainstream, marketable image

of contemporary feminism is that feminism's apex is self-sufficiency within capitalism: women making more money than men. This realized dream is flaunted and celebrated in pop music, hip-hop, and books on women's ascension in business, like Sheryl Sandberg's *Lean In.*

I want to believe in this capitalist dream and revel, especially when my heroes/girl-crushes Beyoncé and Nicki Minaj sing about how hot they are and how amazing they are at making money. There is something radical about black women especially claiming/reclaiming their rightful place in American society, and of course they aren't really singing to me so much as to other black women—as encouragement and solidarity. Feminism means different things to different women.

Yet I can't ignore my suspicion that capitalist materialism is an empty promise to begin with. We are supposed to believe that if enough women have money and power, this will redress fundamental problems of social stratification and oppression, and the implication is that this will make us happy. But does it really?

Of course, I ask this from a place of great privilege, as a white woman who was raised comfortably, went to private schools, and always had enough to eat. On the one hand, renouncing wealth comes from a place of privilege to begin with, and on the other hand, it is a bedrock of Buddhist monastic practice. I want my feminist ideals to align with my Buddhist ones, but they usually don't—especially about money, social stratification, and access to power. It's awkward for me, feeling that I can't be loyal to both at the same time.

When I reflect on the history of Buddhism, it seems to me that the most famous Buddhist masters have been Asian men from wealthy backgrounds who chose to give up their socioeconomic status in order to pursue truth. By my reckoning, the history of Buddhism is primarily a history of formerly wealthy Asian men, and we've inherited that legacy in both Japan and the West for better or for worse. As more and more women make an effort to exhume women's stories and include them in the accepted history of Buddhism, the picture is diversifying a bit. Still, it's hard to ignore that most of the heavy hitters throughout history were rich, educated men.

The historical Buddha is the best example. Before he was the Buddha he was Prince Siddhartha, heir to a kingdom in India. He grew up with all of his needs being met—and his father made an effort to give him all of the best and most beautiful women, clothes, and food, and tried to shelter him from the sad and ugly parts of human existence. But since suffering is inevitable, no amount of beautiful, comfortable things could keep Prince Siddhartha from feeling unsatisfied and from reckoning with old age, sickness, and death. After riding through the city and seeing sick, aging people and corpses, he was shocked out of his complacency and realized his wealth was not going to help him avoid death.

In a way, Siddhartha's material comfort contributed to his deciding to renounce his wealth and his kingdom to live in poverty and practice meditation. The parable of the Buddha's life is useful because he's all of us. We all rely on material comfort to provide a quick fix for our existential problems, and we all try to deny the inevitability of sickness, old age, and death until it's staring us in the face.

Dogen Zenji's story is similar. He came from an aristocratic family and received the best education possible at the time. Dogen's exact familial lineage is debated, though most historians agree he was a descendant of Emperor Murakami—and his writing reveals a high level of education and literary skill. Like the historical Buddha, the course of Dogen's life changed when his mother died when he was eight years old and he was forced to confront the reality of old age, sickness, and death. It's said that when he watched the smoke rise from her burning body, he resolved to become a monk in order to try to understand the "great matter of life and death." At that point, he too gave up his status to live in poverty.

Later in his life, Dogen wrote, "Being poor is being intimate with the Way." I love the parts in Shobogenzo "Gyoji" where Dogen goes on these extended rants/pep talks about poverty, basically saying if we don't have enough rice, we'll make rice gruel, and if we don't have enough rice for gruel, we'll make rice water, and if we don't have rice water, we'll just drink tea. Because we have all this beautiful nature and mountains around us, and like, there are monkeys swinging from the trees, *so what more do you guys want*?! *This is a Zen monastery, not a freakin' IHOP!* To be fair, it's more poetic the way he says it.

For Dogen, being poor is a necessary component to practicing seriously. He says, "To learn the Way, just be poor." This isn't because being poor is more noble, ethical, or socially responsible but because it's easier to concentrate on meditation if you're not worrying about how to make and keep your wealth. For this reason, since the Buddha's time, sanghas have relied on lay supporters—laypeople who believed it was worthwhile for monks to spend all of their time practicing and meditating and who were willing to give money to support that.

I SPENT ABOUT FOUR YEARS not thinking about money, not earning it, and just depending on my sangha for support and practicing. When I left the monastic container, I had to think about how I was going to feed myself and pay for school. And I was incredibly lucky: I received a big grant from the Khyentse Foundation, an awesome organization that gives money to Buddhists from all sects, all over the world, and the aforementioned readers of my blog also donated. It was humbling, encouraging, and terrifying to receive money from strangers who think that what I'm doing is worthwhile.

The year I left Nisodo, I made more money than I ever had in my life. It wasn't much; I was right below the poverty line, which was $11,720 in 2013 according to the U.S. Census Bureau. But even being at the poverty line felt like too much money. Going from having literally no money to being all the way up at the poverty line was a huge change.

"Poverty" by American standards is still pretty damn comfortable. I could do things like choose whether or not I have pancakes, oatmeal, or rice for breakfast. I could buy clothes. For me, that was a whole lot of choice that I didn't have before. From the time I've spent in rural India, it's clear to me that lots of people in the world would love to be living in "poverty" according to American standards.

And I didn't know that I trusted myself with money. When I found out I received the scholarship for school, my first reaction was to check the website to see when I could apply for the scholarship again next year. As in, this money is great, but how can I get even more money out of this? (For the record, my second reaction was to start crying from happiness and gratitude, so I'm not entirely soulless and greedy.) The truth is, I didn't know what "enough" money was. I still don't. I'm not sure that any of us in the Western world do, which is why I tend to want to err on the side of poverty.

I remember having a conversation with Seido Roshi about this once. It went like this:

> *Me*: Do you think I should get a job?
> *Roshi*: Not necessary. Monks don't need money.
> *Me*: Ugh, yes we do. We have to pay the electricity bill.
> *Roshi:* Well, we need a little money.

Most of my conversations with Zen teachers fall into this pattern. Sometimes the roles are reversed, but that doesn't matter. I've narrowed down the teacher-student dynamic to an equation that goes like this:

> *Student/teacher*: Absolute!
> *Teacher/student*: Relative!
> *Student/teacher:* Okay, middle way…

The traditionally Buddhist way of looking at money is

about merit. I think nobody really believes in merit anymore in exactly this form, but people used to think that when you did something "good," like donate money to a temple, this earned you something like invisible merit points that somehow got stored in a cosmic bank account that you could cosmically withdraw from to benefit you in subsequent rebirths. Obviously this is silly—but the more time I spent as a nun chanting for laypeople in their homes, the more I've come to relate to merit like the Beach Boys' song "Good Vibrations." You know: *"I'm picking up good vibrations, she's giving me excitations…"* I would hum this to myself as I rode my bike to people's houses to chant for their deceased ancestors. What was my chanting doing actually? Hell if I know exactly, but it was clear to me it was doing something good. It made them happy, and that made me happy.

Merit is just good stuff that you do. It doesn't get stored in a cosmic bank account in the sky, and we can't necessarily see exactly how or why our good actions matter. But merit itself isn't really a thing. That's why Bodhidharma told the emperor in China that there was "no merit" in the emperor's building large temples. But in some sense, "no merit" also means "lots of merit." The secret of woo-woo Zen language is that in koans and stories, sometimes when someone says "no" or "nothing," this actually means "a lot." Bodhidharma is right; there is no merit. Yet there is good stuff that you do, and it matters very much.

So this man in San Francisco was sending me money. I appreciated it, and I was also wary. I decided to ask my friends at the San Francisco Zen Center if they knew who this weird stalker was who kept sending me money. They confirmed that no, he was not a weird stalker but rather a very sincere practitioner who loved my writing. I checked him out on the internet. He had posted pictures of himself with a new tattoo of the Heart Sutra on his back. His whole back was covered in Chinese characters, and there were pictures of his other tattoos: a dragon, a Dharma wheel, a power button. I looked at that picture of his Heart Sutra tattoo for a long time, finding it both disturbing and oddly fascinating. I saw something of myself in his tattoo: a wholehearted, fully committed embrace of Zen practice, one bordering on obsessive and foolish. I wrote him a thank-you email and asked about the tattoo, to which he responded with a page-long explanation about his tattoo, his hopes and fears, and his relationship to Zen practice. It was more sincere and honest than I had expected from a near stranger. I sent him a postcard next, and things snowballed from there.

I SOMETIMES WONDER how I went from being a nun espousing the merits of lifelong celibacy to a woman with no hair corresponding across an ocean with a man she had never met.

Is it simply that desire got the best of me? Am I a Buddhist cautionary tale? As in, "Look what happens when you leave the convent. It's men with heart sutra tattoos all the way down." In other words, am I proof that the only way to remain "pure" and "virtuous," as the Vinaya texts would have us believe, is to never come into contact with men?

As a feminist, I have been trained to ask, "What is left out of this story? Whose voice is not being heard?" If I tell a story of the benefits of lifelong devotion to celibate monasticism, this leaves out the truth that finding someone to share your life with is a great joy. This leaves out how much we all can grow in intimate partnerships, how deeply healing it is to be fully seen and accepted as who we are by the person we love the most, to work through negotiating boundaries and compromises.

And yet, in telling the story of the wonders of partnership, this leaves out the truth that, as a spiritual practitioner, there is so much to be gained by being single. In polyamorous communities they say, "Love is infinite, but time is not." Even when juggling people and things, you can't have it all.

Of course, when I first started publishing my writing, and then when I started corresponding with this man, I didn't think of it like this. I didn't think at all. I didn't realize that I was profoundly lonely. I just poured myself onto the page, sending my writing out into the world like a message in a bottle. I was looking for someone to answer, hoping for someone to read those messages and understand.

And he did.

21   Don't Move

Sit—even on a stone—for three years.
  —JAPANESE PROVERB

Although the mendicant is no longer upset by the hustle
and bustle of the world, he finds himself prone to the
anxiety engendered by living in the forest.
  —STEPHEN BATCHELOR

THROUGHOUT MY TIME IN JAPAN, my teachers urged me
to keep going and not quit.

"If you really want to learn something deeply," they said,
"it takes time."

And I followed their advice. Even when I acknowledged
parts of the Japanese system were completely broken,
I stayed with it, partly because I trusted my teachers, and
partly because I wanted to see what would happen if I waited.
The more I stayed, the more I saw that they were right, that
things developed very, very slowly.

When I was at Nisodo, Seido Roshi would constantly
remind me of the Japanese proverb "Sit—even on a stone—
for three years." The idea is that if you stay with something
for long enough, even on a stone, good things happen. He
repeated this proverb to me so many times that "three years"

got imprinted on my mind as a good chunk of time, and I think this is why I ended up staying at Nisodo for three years.

Midway into my year of Japanese study, I realized I wanted to go back to the United States. I don't think there was a single defining moment that caused me to want to leave Japan, but like my insights into Buddhist practice, this realization was a gradual one. I became very aware that I wasn't able to do the kinds of things I wanted to do in Japan, and that my options there were limited to either marrying a Japanese man, being an English teacher, owning and running a Zen temple, or serving my teacher tea until he died.

None of these options appealed to me.

Most monks and nuns in Japan are expected to take over a temple after they are finished training, but Seido Roshi had no such expectation for me, and I had little interest in being in charge of a Japanese congregation. Throughout my training I always promised him that I would take care of him when he died, and this is still my intention, but after nearly six years of living in Japan, by the time I was twenty-eight, I felt ready to leave for a long time.

DURING THE YEAR I WAS STUDYING at Nanzan University, I would go back to Toshoji for sesshin or to help with important ceremonies. One time when I was there visiting, I approached my Dharma sister, a forty-year-old Australian nun who, like me, had lived in Japanese monasteries for several years. I forget what exactly we were doing or what prompted my question—but I remember we were wearing robes. In any event, I walked up to her and asked, "Would you say that 95 percent of your practice here is endurance?"

She looked at me, expressionless, and said with her stoic, deadpan Australian accent, "99 percent."

Endurance—or patience, if I'm being generous—has always been a big part of my practice in Japan. In some way, at least, I think it is for people practicing Zen anywhere. We sit with the instruction not to move, and we do this with varying degrees of success through pain, stiffness, itchiness, boredom, restlessness, heat, cold, nihilism…oh, the list goes on! We feel bored and keep sitting anyway. Our legs hurt and we keep sitting.

Uchiyama Roshi wrote that if we cannot sit zazen, simply waiting is a good enough substitute. Because, if I'm really honest, a lot of my zazen is just sitting and waiting for the bell to ring. (God, that sounds horrible. Am I doing this all wrong?)

Waiting and patience are a big part of Zen practice for anybody. Yet I also know that there's a particular kind of endurance reserved for foreign women within Japanese monastic institutions; this is because the people we interact with in the monastery on a daily basis will inevitably treat us like servants, at worst—and at best, treat us like daughters or hapless yet lovable younger sisters.

Sawaki Kodo Roshi wrote of Zen that it "is not for changing the external world. It is for transforming our eyes and ears, our habitual ways of perceiving and thinking." One of the most fundamentally empowering developments I've had over the last years here is the realization—not merely intellectually, but actually embodied on a daily basis—that my own individual effort and work is what is most important. Whether or not anyone else thinks I am lazy or spoiled or incompetent or too American or too emotional or whatever other insult or judgment people can think of, what matters most is my own work and my own practice. No one else can practice or live for me, so looking outside and critiquing other people—from very real social injustices to personality flaws—doesn't really help me so much. A better use of my time is to focus on learning, studying, and embodying the things I have the capacity to learn, study, and embody. It has been wonderful to develop practice that doesn't really depend on what's going on around me. And yet, of course, it can be exhausting.

I did get exhausted. I got exhausted when there were no avenues to register complaints about real imbalances of power; when I was denied work I was just as qualified as or more qualified than others to do; when only the men were allowed to sleep in the zendo while women slept in normal rooms; when people told me Japanese have different internal organs than Americans. The list goes on. For the most part, I took these tiny microaggressions and tried to let them slide. I tried to focus on my own breathing, on my own work, on sweeping and drying dishes and weeding. I tried to not look up or around. I believe there is liberation in that. Sometimes there would be moments when I was enraged and exhausted for so long, and then a spaciousness developed and I could let whatever was happening go. I felt light and free. I could go back to weeding. I could just weed or sweep and that was enough. And sometimes I was only exhausted and enraged.

Both experiences happened. Often.

As I've mentioned, at most Zen monasteries in Japan,

and in the West now too, before new monks and nuns are allowed to enter a practice period, they are required to sit a trial period known as tangaryo. In tangaryo in Japan, you sit zazen all day without moving for a week, breaking only for meals and the bathroom. Since half or full lotus can be uncomfortable enough for a forty-five-minute period, doing this for a week straight can be agonizing.

After I ordained, before I was going to start my tangaryo at the monastery, I asked Seido Roshi, "What do I do if I have to move?" A week seemed like a really long time, and I had heard horror stories about people digging their nails into their palms and drawing blood in order to keep on enduring the zazen posture.

"You can't move," he said.

"But what if I really have to move?"

"Don't move," he reiterated.

"But what if I really, really have to move?"

"Well, then you move."

It sounds so simple when it's laid out like that, doesn't it?

We take up the posture of not moving, and we don't move, and don't move, despite the pain and itchiness and restlessness, until we simply must move, and then we do. This is true with most things. With any sort of commitment—a friendship, a romantic relationship, a marriage, a monastery, a period of academic study, a job, a diet, an exercise regime, a forty-minute zazen period. We try our best to stay in one place, where we promised to stay, until we can't anymore, and then we move.

I sat with the "itch" of my life in Japan for a very long

time. I sat with it until I felt no neurosis about moving. Sometimes staying in one place and being patient is right, and sometimes moving is right too, when it's the only thing left to do.

22   The Hardest and Best Way

The beauty of the impostor syndrome is you vacillate
between extreme egomania and a complete feeling of:
"I'm a fraud! Oh God, they're on to me! I'm a fraud!"
So you just try to ride the egomania when it comes and
enjoy it, and then slide through the idea of fraud.

   —TINA FEY, *BOSSYPANTS*

When we abandon the east and try to hide
away in the west, the west is also not without
its circumstances.

   —DOGEN ZENJI, SHOBOGENZO *"RAIHAI TOKUZUI"*

MIDWAY THROUGH MY STAY AT NISODO it became clear
that I would do Dharma transmission. For Japanese monks
and nuns, transmission is practical: it secures the ability to
own a temple, and thus, the ability to live. From the other
nuns, I received very clear, very explicit messages about how
my next step should be transmission. For example, in Nisodo
everyone takes a sewing class in which we sequentially sew
a chopstick case, a rakusu, three miniature okesas called
san-e, a seven-row okesa for everyday use, and finally, a nine-
row okesa for after transmission. Because Seido Roshi's lineage uses blue okesas for beginners, I had made the decision

to sew a blue okesa instead of a black one, which is the more common novice color. After I finished the blue, seven-row okesa, I told Aoyama Roshi that I wanted to sew a black okesa next. I remember I was her assistant at the time, so I was sitting at the head of the table below her and to the left. She scowled at me. I could probably feel her scowl from across a room, but sitting next to her it was even stronger.

"Why would you sew a black okesa? You should sew a brown one."

As if I hadn't internalized the message, later at my shuso hossenshiki, my sewing teacher gave me a bolt of brown fabric as a congratulations gift.

"After your hossenshiki, you do transmission," she explained, as if reminding a fully grown adult to lock the car door after getting out.

Soon thereafter, Seido Roshi suggested we do Dharma transmission so that I could qualify to take the test needed to become a goeka (Buddhist hymn) teacher. I thought this was a terrible reason to do transmission and told him so, quite angrily, and I think I may literally have stomped out of the room and slammed the door.

For several years I couldn't be around him for more than a few hours without being overwhelmed with anger. Being in the same space with him was like walking through a minefield, only the minefield was my own emotional terrain. I tried to go back to Toshoji sometimes, but it became only more difficult, not less. Given our history, I thought it was too messy and complicated to continue with him. If he loved me, how could I receive transmission from him? Wasn't that all kinds of wrong—immoral, impractical, painful, psychologically damaging? Didn't it diminish the meaning of transmission? And so, toward the end of my studies at Nanzan, I asked Aoyama Roshi officially to be my teacher. Seido Roshi agreed to do the paperwork as long as I asked Aoyama Roshi personally and got permission to change (in Japan, monks and nuns are "registered" with a certain teacher, and switching teachers is a somewhat complicated, bureaucratic process).

I put on my best robes, bought a large bagful of cakes and other gifts, and went to visit Aoyama Roshi at Nisodo. I even secured a translator so that I could communicate my desire with her effectively. Nervously, I made my request.

She thought for a moment and smiled, embarrassed. "But I'm so old," she said. "I'm going to die soon." I tried again to explain the situation to her, how I couldn't practice with him any more. "You should be grateful to him," she said finally. "He has spent so much time and effort and money to take care of you."

I left the room shaking and immediately ducked into a dark hallway, where I pressed my forehead against the wall and cried. I felt betrayed and devastated. For the hundredth or thousandth time in my stay in Japan, I thought that what was being asked of me was too difficult. How could I possibly do what she was asking?

Looking back on it, I'm pretty clear she didn't really understand why I was asking, and I didn't have the language to talk about it. I couched everything in vague terms, and that's what she heard, so of course she said no.

But part of me likes to think that she did understand, and said no anyway.

I RESPECTED AOYAMA ROSHI.

What I had learned from three years of practicing with her is that she always recommends the hardest and the best way, whether it is a ceremonial form, training method, or life decision. Human beings don't usually like to do the hardest and best way, and although the hardest way isn't necessarily the best way, the best way can often be the hardest.

Because I respected her, because I had seen countless times how doing the hardest and the best way in my own life made me grow and become more solid, I decided to try to be grateful to Seido Roshi. What she was teaching me, over and over again, was to deal with the life and the karma that was right in front of me. Whenever I tried to escape my life and my karma, she always directed me back to it. At the time, I often resented this, because it was so hard, and the things in my life were painful. But that was her teaching. Your life is your material. It is the ground of your awakening. There is only your life to work with—your own suffering. So use it! It can all be used. Your sadness. Ringing bells. Stirring soup. Your shame and lust and regret. The towel where you dry your hands after you use the toilet. What other place is there to practice?

So I said yes to Seido Roshi's transmission.

And with it, all of our karma.

ABOUT A YEAR INTO MY STAY AT NISODO, my mother sent me a book called *Inner Gold: Understanding Psychological Projection*, by a Jungian psychologist named Robert Johnson. He describes how all people have "inner gold," the best parts of ourselves—our wit, intelligence, kindness, and talent—but that for most people, carrying this gold ourselves is too hard. It's hard to carry our own gold because the gold is so heavy, and so we find other people to carry it for us for a time. Robert Johnson calls this process of handing over our gold to someone else *psychological projection*, which has kind of become a buzzword in Buddhist communities, but I think for good reason.

Sharon Salzberg wrote that *bright faith* is like falling in love, and I think many of us can relate to her description of her first encounter with Buddhism. In her book *Faith* she writes:

> I arrived in Bodhgaya in late December 1970 and fell in love. I fell in love with the meditation teachers I found there, and with the community of students who gathered around them. I fell in love with the Buddha's teachings. I fell in love with the place. Even discomfort and uncertainty didn't tarnish the romance.... This state of love-filled delight in possibilities and eager joy at the prospect of actualizing them is known in Buddhism as bright faith. Bright faith goes beyond merely claiming that possibility for oneself to immersing oneself in it. With bright faith we feel exalted as we are lifted out of our normal sense of insignificance, thrilled as we no longer feel lost and alone.

I know this was true for me. I came to Japan and fell in love—with an old temple, with the mountains, with my teacher, with the practice, even with the cold and the pain. And like most new students, I handed over all my gold. Robert Johnson says when we hero worship, we hand over our gold to someone else until we can get strong enough to carry it ourselves. But eventually we have to take it back. Taking back your own gold can be painful because sometimes the people we've given our gold to—the people we fall in love with—don't want to give the gold back. Sometimes we have to slam the door to announce we are leaving. It's difficult to do in a kind and respectful way.

Dharma transmission means a lot of different things to a lot of people, but for me it meant getting my gold back. This was the choice I made after several years of pain and struggle, and the actual transmission ceremony helped reinforce my decision to stand on my own two feet. In his book on projection, Robert Johnson actually suggests that people (usually a therapist and patient) can do a ceremony in which they exchange gold; he describes buying a small amount of gold and giving it to a patient who worshipped him to the extent that the patient could not make progress in therapy. Giving back gold (or reclaiming it) in Buddhist practice is important as well.

In the beginning, it's necessary to fall in love with a practice and a teacher in a certain sense, because this helps us listen to and learn from the teachings, but in the end we take back our gold so that we can hold it ourselves; we understand that it's our own responsibility to act as our best selves as much as possible, to uphold the teachings the best way we can, to give light rather than take it.

In this sense, mature Buddhist practice is actually the opposite of falling in love. When we fall in love, we give the best part of ourselves to something external, thinking it will change us. When we practice well we know that the burden of transformation is really on us, and we act from this place. So practice is really the opposite of falling in love.

But loving and falling in love are completely different. bell hooks defines love as "the action we take on behalf of our own or another's spiritual growth." Speaking about love as an action or a choice is powerful. Martin Luther King Jr. said, "I have decided to love," and in saying this he pointed out that he could have decided something else. He could have chosen not to love.

Practice is like this as well. Practice is an action and a choice. It's a choice, moment by moment, to do things in the best way you know how, to meet everything with the best self that shows up. In Zen we say "the student must stand on the teacher's shoulders." In an ideal world this would mean that the student has a greater level of realization than the teacher. I'm sure my teacher has had more "enlightenment experiences" than I, and he is about fifty billion times more qualified than I to run a monastery, for example. Yet I stand on his shoulders. I do this when I draw boundaries and know what is good and true for me while also respecting him, his tradition, and being grateful for his presence in my life. That is the hardest and best way: to love without falling in love, to love with boundaries and wisdom, and with the generosity that comes from that defined place.

23   Too Late Now,
It's Already on the Blackboard

In the ocean, there is a place called the Dragon-Gate,
where vast waves rise incessantly. Without fail, all
fish once having passed through this place become
dragons.... The way of Zen monks is also like this.
Although it is not a special place, if you enter a
monastery, without fail you will become a Buddha
or a patriarch.

  —DOGEN ZENJI, *SHOBOGENZO ZUIMONKI*

But if these years have taught me anything it is this: you
can never run away. Not ever. The only way out is in.

  —JUNOT DIAZ, *THE BRIEF AND WONDROUS LIFE OF OSCAR WAO*

So I SEWED A BROWN NINE-ROW OKESA.

I say this pretty casually, but it took a small army of
monks and nuns helping me. The okesa is incredibly beautiful, and I feel comfortable saying this because I had very
little to do with it. My sewing teacher at Nisodo, Doko
Sensei, gave me a bolt of thin, nearly translucent brown
silk, and soft brown cotton for the lining. Two European
priests helped me sew the front during a weeklong sewing
intensive at Toshoji, and a seventy-year-old Japanese nun

sewed almost the entire back lining for me. All of those sewers were impeccable, professional-grade sewers, much more skilled than I am. In the past I had sewed an okesa entirely by myself, each and every stitch, and I'm proud of that effort, but this time around, the okesa was a literal patchwork made by friends and benefactors. Like my practice itself, it was stitched together by dozens of benefactors from around the world. I couldn't have done it alone.

Usually we think of "our practice" as something that we own and control, but the fact is it is a product of innumerable causes and conditions we can't see. It is aided by our parents, friends, teachers, community, donors, and so many others. When I speak of my transmission now, it's difficult and bittersweet. On the one hand, it's something that I personally received. It's my name on the lineage chart, and no one else's. On the other hand, I was enabled to do this practice and receive this transmission because of my teachers and the other older monks and nuns who helped train me. They say it takes a village to raise a child, and in my case, it definitely took a village—multiple villages!—to get me where I am now: kind people who taught me Japanese, how to cook, how to bow, sew, chant, and sit. So while I feel unqualified and undeserving to wear this brown robe as some marker of my individual efforts, I do want to wear it because I respect and love the people who helped me—both literally and metaphorically—become the person who could, actually, be qualified to wear that robe.

The night before the transmission ceremony, I cried and tried to back out of it. I think "sobbed" is a more appropriate word. At the last minute, I finally realized what was happening, the weight of it, and how I was too small and too young. "You want to quit?" Seido Roshi asked me. "You can't quit now. Your ceremony is written on the blackboard." There's a blackboard in the monastery where the calendar and list of daily events are written.

"But I'm too young!" I protested. I was twenty-nine.

"Dogen was twenty-eight," he reminded me.

"But I am not Dogen. Dogen was enlightened."

"Eh," he said. "It's okay."

The ceremony takes a week. Every morning I sat zazen and did morning service with the rest of the monks and nuns, but after service I took a small handheld incense burner and went around to each altar in the monastery, chanting and offering incense. I then returned to my room and did a series of bows and chanting in front of something called the dragon scroll—a special scroll each monk and nun is given when they ordain. During the day I copied the transmission documents onto silk; there are three different kinds of documents, each with different symbolism. The final day there is a more formal ceremony with many bows, which takes place late at night in a room covered in red fabric.

After we finished I had two days left. On those two days I officiated morning service for the first time in the six years since I set foot in Japan. I had watched Seido Roshi do the morning service so many times that I thought it would feel scary and unnatural, but it felt completely natural. Everyone was happy. Soen-san, the wife of a local temple priest who had been visiting the monastery since before I came to Japan, who had first met me as a twenty-three-year-old layperson with long hair, a nasty temper, and a bad habit of sleeping through morning work, gave me a big hug after morning service. She was the only other person at the monastery besides Seido Roshi who had known me from the very beginning.

"You did so well today," she said, smiling.

She took off a *juzu*, a string of Buddhist prayer beads, from around her wrist and pressed it into my hand. "You became a great woman," she said. She repeated herself several times, never using the word *person* or *adult*, but always *woman*. "Please come back and teach the other foreigners," she said finally.

I promised I would.

I started to feel very jazzed about receiving transmission, and I guess my arrogance showed. "Don't announce," Seido Roshi told me. "Keep it a secret for ten years, like Daikan Eno." Several months later I would call him in confusion.

"What color okesa am I supposed to be wearing?" I would ask.

"You can wear brown," he said nonchalantly.

"But you said I shouldn't tell anyone I have transmission."

"No, I meant don't show the transmission documents to anyone."

Of course, I knew this wasn't what he had said originally, but it's possible he flat out forgot, so I let him have his "alternative facts." But of course in the moment, I took his words very seriously. I made plans to practice at Green Gulch Farm, a Zen monastery and farm in Northern California, for a few months, and asked to work in the kitchen. This was partly because I like kitchen work and also because Daikan Eno, the Sixth Patriarch, worked silently and humbly in the kitchen. I suspected it would be good, quiet practice, a remedy for my big head.

Transmission is still in many ways an unresolved question for me. What does it mean to wear this brown robe, especially as a twenty-nine-year-old?

It's relatively easy to write these lofty things about psychological projection and getting my gold back, but on a lived, daily level, it is still hard to carry my gold sometimes. I still have doubts about my abilities and qualifications, and I doubt my own tradition. Perhaps they are the same doubts.

What I do know is that my teacher trusts me.

THE WEEK BEFORE I RECEIVED TRANSMISSION, before I left Japan, a team from the local news came to do a segment on temples in that area. Seido Roshi volunteered me to be interviewed about zazen and lead instructions in Japanese to the local news team. I spent a few hours studying the specific Japanese words I would need for zazen instructions, words like *palm*, *thigh*, and *cosmic mudra* (I mean, how often do I need that in daily conversation?). The local news filmed me entering the zendo, getting up on the *tan*, the raised platform, and sitting zazen. Then they interviewed me about why I sit zazen and the "meaning" of practice. I struggled and floundered to explain, in Japanese, something that I think needs very little explanation even in English.

The night after my transmission ceremony, Seido Roshi and I watched the news segment together. I had filled his room with flowers: tulips, cherry blossoms, and late-winter camellias, and I gave him a rakusu that my mother and I had sewn for him. We sat on the floor, drinking ginger tea, and watched the DVD on his laptop. I thought it was painfully embarrassing, hearing myself try to explain "seeing yourself" in Japanese. Seido Roshi had in many ways given me an impossible task, a task I was entirely unqualified for.

"Very good!" he said, beaming with happiness.

I grimaced in embarrassment.

And, you know, if it had been the national news, then he might not have asked me to explain the meaning of practice and zazen on camera, in Japanese. But the local news?

Yeah, he trusted me with that.

24   Coming Home

In this here place, we flesh; flesh that weeps, laughs;
flesh that dances on bare feet in grass. Love it. Love it
hard.... Love it and the beat and beating heart.... Hear
me now, love your heart. For this is the prize.

—TONI MORRISON

For so long here without worldly attachments,
I have renounced literature and writing;
I may be a monk in a mountain temple,
Yet still moved in seeing gorgeous blossoms
Scattered by the spring breeze,
And hearing the warbler's lovely song—
Let others judge my meager efforts.

—DOGEN ZENJI, *THE ZEN POETRY OF DOGEN*

I KNOW MY TEACHER DID NOT SPRAY ME with magical enlightenment juice when we did transmission, but for at least a month after the ceremony I had tremendous clarity about what I wanted from life and what my priorities were. I knew, for example, that I wanted to write a book. I also knew I wanted to be in love—that I needed to be in love. All the neurosis I had over whether or not to remain unmarried or celibate had evaporated.

I stayed in the San Francisco Zen Center for two weeks before moving into Green Gulch. One of the first things I did after arriving was contact Gensan—the man with the Heart Sutra tattoo. I had brought him a calligraphy from Japan. Ostensibly this was to say thank you for his donations, but secretly I wanted to get to know him. The first week I was at Zen Center I gave him the calligraphy, and then he asked me to dinner. To this day he insists he wasn't hitting on me, that I was just an author he admired, but at this point in life I just assume that if a man asks me to dinner, he wants to kiss me and touch my skin. Because if he just wanted to chat, he would just invite me to coffee or to a country fair. That's how dating works, right?

AT SAN FRANCISCO ZEN CENTER, there is a policy called "the six-month rule," which forbids students from forming new sexual relationships within the first six months of residency. The rule also extends to residents who have lived there longer, prohibiting them from initiating a romantic relationship with a new student. This includes telling a new student you find them attractive or are interested in them. I wasn't sure if we were breaking a rule or not, and I didn't want to break any rules. But what was the rule against going to dinner with someone you liked? I said yes.

We planned to meet on a Sunday, when we both had a day off. I suggested walking through Golden Gate Park before dinner, and oddly, he requested that we not meet at a certain entrance to the park.

"Is that where your rival gang hangs out?" I asked.

"If by rival gang you mean my ex-wife, her new boy, and their baby, then yes."

He was thirty-nine, ten years older than I, with a failed marriage. He'd had a child when he was a teenager that he'd given up for adoption, and he spoke openly about struggling with mental illness. By normal standards, this is supposed to be a turnoff, but if you've paid attention throughout this book, you might understand by now that the words *supposed to* don't really register with me.

If someone tells me I'm not supposed to do something, or that it's bad for me, I have to stick my face in it so I know for myself. I liked that his flaws and wounds were out in the open, like the tattoos on his arms, like the scars on his deltoids from where he'd dragged a knife over his skin a decade earlier. He was open and honest about everything in his past, and he seemed simultaneously broken and whatever the opposite of broken is. He was successful at his job and dedicated to Buddhism. He spoke sincerely and gently.

We walked all over Golden Gate Park, past the Academy of Science, past the Japanese Tea Garden, the Conservatory of Flowers, around Stow Lake, and through patches of land that were untended and overgrown, filled with fallen tree branches and leaves. It was here, surrounded by the skeletons of dead trees, that he told me about his ten-year marriage and divorce, about the many, many times his wife had cheated on him and how he'd stayed.

We started talking every day, and after lights out we would go walking through Hayes Valley, or sit on the bench in Alamo Square Park, looking at the night sky and the famous row of Victorian houses. We did cute things like sit in the sunshine and eat ice cream and talk for hours. We held hands but never kissed because that would be breaking a rule and we were trying very, very hard not to do this, even though we were crazy about each other, and who were we kidding with all the hand holding?

Eventually we decided to tell the abbot what was happening because I still fear authority for some reason. Gensan wrote the abbot an email about me so detailed and forthright and sincere it was painful.

I left the Zen Center for a few days and stayed with my parents to get ready to move to Green Gulch. During that time, Gensan and I had a meeting where the abbot asked me embarrassingly pointed questions about my past relationships and my plans for the future, and then I waved my hands in front of him and said, "These are not the droids you are looking for, and we are not breaking the six-month rule."

And my Jedi powers worked!

I WROTE MY SENIOR THESIS IN COLLEGE ABOUT LOVE, and I've thought and written a lot about it since then, but it's still one of the most difficult things to describe in writing. It's nearly impossible to compete with the experience or describe how invincible love makes me feel. After so many years living as a nun, practicing around other nuns, I'm amazed at how easily and naturally I slipped back into being in love—walking around the city holding hands, feeling like we were the only two people in existence, hours spent in bed, trying and failing to get up and get dressed, nights bleeding into mornings that turned into afternoons.

When I was in college I wrote a love poem called "Republic of Bed." It was about how being in love is like living in a despotic kingdom with a population of two, which doesn't grant exit visas. After all my discipline and seeking, there I was again, trapped in the Republic of Bed.

"You can't hold two things with one hand," I told Gensan, echoing my teacher's advice to me about love and practice in the moments when it seemed impossible to balance a monastic schedule with being in relationship.

"I have big hands," he said.

I am grateful for his stubbornness, because it turned out I could actually hold both things, in the same way I have learned how to hold gratitude and anger and sadness at the same time. My capacity to hold many contradictory things had grown. I wasn't actually trapped in the Republic of Bed.

I moved to Green Gulch, eased into practice at a new community, and found some kind of strange balance. Gensan would come up on weekends to stay with me, and I would wake up on time, at 4:30 A.M., and peel myself from his skin to go the zendo to sit zazen. I shaved my head, wore robes, and worked in the kitchen during the day.

For the first time in my life, there were people my age who spoke my same language, who were interested in the same things as I. I worked hard in the kitchen and followed the schedule. After lunch I had a break and would walk down through the garden or to the beach, appreciating the green hills and flowers around me.

ONE AFTERNOON, while walking down to the beach, down the narrow road lined with crabapple trees, I felt a strange tightness in my chest. I thought it might be heartburn or something more sinister.

It took me a while to recognize the feeling that was

occurring, but then I realized: this is joy. I hadn't felt that in so long, I had almost forgotten the word. It was so strong it eclipsed everything for a moment. There were other sensations mixed in: love, elation at being back in California, my home among the eucalyptus trees and the California poppies of my childhood, joy at being surrounded by green, satisfaction at having arrived at closure with my teacher and with Japan.

I knew the feeling wouldn't last, but I didn't care. I held the feeling in my palm, like a ray of sunshine that was fading, and I laughed out loud at how simple joy was.

Afterword

If you have understood, then this is not God. If you were able to understand, then you have understood something else instead of God. If you were able to understand even partially, then you have deceived yourself with your own thoughts.

—SAINT AUGUSTINE

To say "Buddha" means to say "Dharma." To say "Dharma" means the truth, which is uncertainty. So the Buddha means "uncertainty."

—AJAHN AMARO

IF MY SIX YEARS IN JAPAN was like being a seed planted deeply into very dense soil, a soil in which I couldn't grow but could absorb nutrients, moving to America was like being transferred to a greenhouse.

When I moved back a lot of things happened very fast. Earlier that year I had applied to graduate school to study Japanese Buddhism, and in the spring I got into UC Berkeley, Harvard Divinity School, and University of Southern California. Eventually both UC Berkeley and USC offered me enough money in scholarships to cover tuition; USC also threw in a stipend on top. I committed to move to Los

Angeles to complete a master's in East Asian studies, where I hoped to translate Aoyama Roshi's writing into English.

After a couple of not-so-difficult conversations, Gensan agreed to follow me "anywhere."

This included Los Angeles, apparently.

THEN I SIGNED A CONTRACT with Wisdom Publications to write this book. Ever since leaving Nisodo I'd been trying, in various ways, to write about my doubts and understanding—and really, about my process of becoming an adult—without being too sad or too self-important, which is the ever-present specter of personal writing, and finally I found a writing style that actually worked. This book flowed out of two years of old writing and new narrative.

MEANWHILE, I had moved to Green Gulch Farm and was working in the kitchen. I attended meetings and classes. I saw my friends and family on the weekend, and I went to dokusan with the Green Gulch teachers. This felt somewhat disingenuous, but I was trying to embody the form of being a student, for their benefit as much as mine. And also, I think there is never a point at which we stop being students. I tried to follow my teacher's advice and not tell anyone about transmission, although slowly and inevitably it seeped into conversations. I'm not very good at secrets.

Gensan and my mother sewed me a brown rakusu, the color of a teacher. I hadn't made a brown rakusu myself yet, and it was another piece of sewing I felt unqualified to wear that someone else had made for me. We went to a

Zen Center event and I wore it, not because I felt qualified to wear it, but because he *and my mother* had spent hours making it for me. I think it's odd and delightful that after all of my years of home leaving, my first brown rakusu—the symbol of my being qualified to teach Zen Buddhism—was made for me by my mother and boyfriend, the people I'm most attached to in the world.

"Why don't you start your own temple?" The abbess of Green Gulch asked me in a private discussion.

"I want to," I said, "but I think I'm too young."

"How young is too young?"

It's an interesting question. How young is too young? What does that mean? Too young for what? To teach what?

"I think you will have to do things in your own way," she advised me.

"No one has ever told me that before. I've only been told to follow tradition."

"To be a true bodhisattva in the world, we have to do things in our own way."

ONE NIGHT GENSAN TOOK ME OUT to Greens Restaurant, a famous gourmet vegetarian restaurant that used to be owned by the San Francisco Zen Center. I wore a green satin dress, black high heels, and the only nice pair of earrings I had kept throughout my ordination and years of simplicity in the monastery. It was a four-course meal, and I drank beer and laughed, feeling very much in love and how a normal twenty-nine-year-old woman is supposed to feel, sitting across from a man who loves her, looking forward to a blossoming professional career—confident and happy.

The next morning during zazen, sitting silently in the predawn dark, a question broke through my stillness and contentment: What about the great matter of life and death?

The question Dogen went to China for, the question I went to Japan to solve, ever since Dave died, even though I didn't have words for it then. What about the great matter of life and death? What can I take with me when I die?

I still had these heady questions, but underneath them all was a simpler one: How can I be happy? What does it mean to live a good life?

I felt tremendous gratitude for that question, how it cut ruthlessly through my feelings of material success, through all of my hard-earned satisfaction, even through the love I knew was real, and good. The question felt different this time around—less pained, less panicked. Beneath the question was still that unbreakable quality I found at my worst moments in Japan, the strength that was an unstoppable force pushing me upward, like an underground stream. I know everyone can find that inner stream of resilience. We can conjure it from inside ourselves if we are skilled enough magicians, and it can push our lives up out of the ground. We can make our own strength, and we can make our questions into strength. I knew that even if I never answered my question, I wanted to keep asking it.

I've kept my question close to me, letting it drive me forward.

Acknowledgments

I've noticed that in acknowledgment sections, it's customary for an author to thank their agent first and their spouse last. But since I do not have an agent, I think I will thank my partner up front. This book would not have been possible without Gensan; you are my first reader and quite literally my biggest fan. It's hard to quantify how much you have supported me, both physically and emotionally, while I was writing and editing this. Sometimes I think when I first started my blog, I was calling out to you across the ocean, and I'm so grateful you heard me and called back. I'm super stoked to have married you.

Thank you to Josh Bartok for being a patient and skilled midwife to the screaming, bloody, beautiful thing that is this book, for coaxing me out of pathological self-deprecation (almost), and for being both kind and firm at the right times. Working with a good editor is a rare and wonderful thing, and I am grateful for your time, help, and talent.

To Brad Warner for being the first person to ever call me a "terrific writer": you believed in me and my writing when no one else did, and you broadcast me to the world, which was terrifying but set me on the course to write this book. Thank you for being my friend and for encouraging me to teach when no one else did. I still think you're really wrong about feminism, though.

Thank you to James Ford for planting the idea in my head to write this book, for introducing me to his publishers, for being generally kind and supportive, and for many delicious dinners.

Thank you to Koun Franz for being my Dharma brother from another mother and the first editor I worked with, albeit at *Buddhadharma* magazine. Thank you for encouraging me to ask questions, to ask and live in "I don't know."

Thank you to all the nuns at Nisodo—too many to name, and I have changed most of your names in this book—but especially Eko-san, Kito-sensei, Hosai-san, and Myokyo-san, who were all wonderful teachers and *senpai*. I miss you all.

To my teachers: Aoyama Roshi, you cannot read English, but I want to say thank you for breaking me down and putting me back together again. You have taught me everything I know about how to practice well. I am so grateful.

To Seido Roshi, for inspiring me to ordain; for five years of feeding and clothing me; for my health insurance and immigration forms; for buying me winter clothes; for giving me my first oryoki bowl, my first rakusu, my robes, my kimonos, a zendo and a cushion when all I wanted to do was sit; and finally, your kotsu and okesa; for all of this, I am grateful. I'm proud of how we try to walk this Buddha Way together.

About the Author

GESSHIN CLAIRE GREENWOOD was born and raised in San Francisco. The child of American Buddhists, she studied abroad in Bodh Gaya, India, where she received temporary ordination in the Burmese Theravada lineage. She spent the majority of her twenties in India and Japan practicing Buddhism, ordaining with Seido Suzuki Roshi in 2010. She received dharma transmission from Suzuki Roshi in 2015, then completed zuise in 2017, granting her the title of "osho," or teacher, within the Soto Zen school. She can be found online at Gesshin.net.

What to Read Next from Wisdom Publications

THE HIDDEN LAMP
Stories from Twenty-Five Centuries of Awakened Women
Edited by Zenshin Florence Caplow
and Reigetsu Susan Moon
Foreword by Zoketsu Norman Fischer

"An amazing collection. This book gives the wonderful feel of the sincerity, the great range, and the nobility of the spiritual work that women are doing and have been doing, unacknowledged, for a very long time. An essential and delightful book."—John Tarrant, author of *The Light Inside the Dark: Zen, Soul, and the Spiritual Life*

PURE HEART, ENLIGHTENED MIND
The Life and Letters of an Irish Zen Saint
Maura O'Halloran

"A grand adventure."—*New York Times* Book Review

HARDCORE ZEN
Punk Rock, Monster Movies, and the Truth About Reality
Brad Warner

"*Hardcore Zen* is to Buddhism what the Ramones were to rock and roll: A clear-cut, no-bulls**t offering of truth."
—Miguel Chen, author of *I Wanna Be Well*

SALTWATER BUDDHA
A Surfer's Quest to Find Zen on the Sea
Jaimal Yogis

"Heartfelt, honest, and deceptively simple. It's great stuff with the words 'Cult Classic' stamped all over it."
—Alex Wade, author of *Surf Nation*

THE WAY OF TENDERNESS
Awakening through Race, Sexuality, and Gender
Zenju Earthlyn Manuel
Foreword by Dr. Charles Johnson

"Manuel's teaching is a thought-provoking, much-needed addition to contemporary Buddhist literature."
—*Publishers Weekly*